Stylistic about Style

First, to my parents: Mohammad and Daulat Siddiqui
then to my siblings and peers, all of who have endlessly and
profoundly influenced me

CONTENTS

STYLISTIC ABOUT STYLE vii
ACKNOWLEDGEMENTS ix
PREFACE xi

i | Introduction 1

ii | FASHION: Aspects, Processes, Thoughts, Methods 23

iii | VIGNETTES 1. Identity 2. Time 3. Inspiration: INS 57

iv | Epilogue 71

v | Author's Note 79

AUTHOR BIO 85

| iii |

Stylistic about Style

Umar Siddiqui

STYLISTIC ABOUT STYLE

Have you ever felt like a hypocrite when someone calls you a trendsetter, because you don't know the specifics of fashion? Other than that, have you struggled to discover and research themes and ideas, namely in fashion? Umar Siddiqui offers a profound look into the world of fashion and how it impacts us. From time and space to vignettes regarding styling and inspiration to marketing terms and research terms like demographics and consumer behavior, this book compels you to go out into the world and make realizations about an art that involves you, physically and mentally.

ACKNOWLEDGEMENTS

In this section, I aim to extend my utmost gratitude who shaped my mind and me and inspired me to invest my time and intrigue in writing and fashion. I assuredly have myriads of people and sources to thank, but I seek to keep it brief and touch upon the people that I whole-heartedly, not just dedicate this book to, but am grateful to. I briefly want to mention my parents and my family in general for their endlessly encouraging and elating comments on my writing, poetry, and fashion choices. See how these intertwine and/ or overlap?

The first person I want to thank is Walt Disney. He one of the people that routinely inspires me and posthumously as well. Though I've obviously never made his acquaintance (at least not in person), I want to say I do have a very vested and personal connection to him and his films. It is with great pride that I call myself a Disney nut, Disney Geek, or Disnerd; what have you! The most prominent and recurrent reason I cite Mr. Disney is that his philosophies cohere on my life. I think being timeless, but not only timeless, but opposing a lot of facets of growing up is key to writing about artistic mediums like fashion. I am endlessly and inexplicably drawn to Disney; it is one of my utmost livelihoods and passion, paralleling fashion for me.

Walt Disney is an icon of American imagination, and he and Mr. Mouse (Mickey Mouse), are my heroes. I want to also bring in the innumerably countless and seminal fashion figures and thinkers that have sept intractably and unavoidably into this project. Sure, my educators and education are to thank, but on a wider level, Diana Vreeland, Grace Coddington, Ralph Lauren, Donna Karan, Karl Lagerfeld, and Jerry Lorenzo are to thank! Then there are Pakistani designers like Omer Farooq, Humayun Alamgir, and Deepak Perwani, Nilofer Shahid, and

Sania Maskatiya to thank! I also want to say media and entertainment in general, as well as popular culture, are largely entities I want to cite here.

    Aside from family, friends, and peers who have been infinitely encouraging and have appropriately engaged with my fashion, my writing, my Disney obsession, etc., there are people that have encouraged my fashion sense and encouraged me to never stop.

PREFACE

According to Agnes Rocamora and Anneke Smelik in the Introduction for *Thinking through Fashion* (2015), "To think – to develop, test, and evaluate theories – is an act that occurs within a certain context" (p. 7.) This book will indispensably employ the utilizations of theory in research and exemplify who the two work with each other and complement each other. Rocamora and Smelik (2015) state that evaluating theories occurs within certain contexts. Context, as we will see with geography, is irrevocably and tirelessly involved in both influencing research and situating it. They go on to say, "theorizing does not happen in a vacuum" (Rocamora & Smelik, 2015, p. 7.) This restates and reiterates the notion that these are endless intrinsic and extrinsic factors that permeate the study (of fashion) and the ruminating on it and investigating of it.

To think through fashion, we will do better to realize it exists, not just in many orientations, directions and dimensions, but that it exists on multiple planes. The planes are spaces in which fashion has an interaction with us, nurturing us while we nourish it. We gain ideas from these planes, and we can see the factors that distinguish these planes. The planes intersect and interact, giving a more nuanced exposure to fashion for us.

Even though I am writing about fashion and reflecting on it, it is increasingly hard. Its volatile nature makes it this way. It is evergreen; it is ever-present. It is infinitely dynamic as it has endless ins and outs. It is marked by countless, unnamable symbolisms and allegories. Writing about fashion innately constitutes telling varying levels of stories. Writing about fashion is an insanely, enormously demanding tasks that requires insight and retrospection but also hypervigilance and proactiveness and a keen, artistic eye. It parallels and imitates arts so many times and in so many iterations that this seeps into the writing. It parallels design and is, itself, an inextricably artistic process. It makes the writer feel elated, alleviated, and changed and like they have made a tremendous contribution to the art and fashion world and critical, philosophical world at large. Its nature can be considered a blank slate; it can be looked at as innocuous—but it definitely has a side that can encourage us to look at it more vigilantly, constructively, and critically. The aim of this is not to be nitpicky but to be productive, and the experience can be eye-opening. In experiencing fashion, we feel it is malleable, subjective, and volatile—yielding a multitude of perspectives and experiences. It is not monolithic or tailored to one person, and can be experienced passively (with restriction, without thought or conviction) or actively (openly and with insight and opinion.) It can be experienced in a multitude of directions and dimensions as well.

Just as a quick but very necessary aside, I would say my vision for this book is, at first glance, cliché; I want my readers to get something out of it. What I want is for them to have a perspective and adopt one of their own. I have my views, and I sincerely hope all of the intricacies and nuances I allude to with my sources here, are intriguing to read; I genuinely hope this book acts as an authentic window into myriad facets of the fashion milieu, especially of today. Writing such a book does require hypervigilance and proactiveness; it is worth it as it alleviates me (and reading it hopefully alleviates you) and I feel like I have genuinely made a contribution to my own psyche (feeling elated and capable) and to the art world and fashion world and cultural world. Fashion is infinitely ever-present and dynamic; it exists everywhere and has evolutionary ins-and-outs. It manifests itself everywhere and is in a state of constant and unceasing flux, as it grows and changes very sporadically; it grows with different speeds at different times in its cycles and livelihood.

Often and unfathomable and inexplicable entity at large due to its weighted, idiosyncratic, and convoluted nature, fashion is challenging to navigate. I honestly think that the more you know fashion, the more you can challenge your mind. You can make realizations about the roles and positionalities it gives. Within these, there are symbols and cultural language. The symbolic facets of fashion speak directly to its creative nature. We can talk about the dramaturgical theory (which will be covered) in its roles and symbolic interactionism (which will be covered too.) Fashion's symbols are plentiful and all around us; they can be embodied or abstract. The symbols possess meanings, as fashion, at every level, has underlying meanings (the ones you do not readily see.) Symbolic capital can be defined as nonmaterial resources that give us prestige and influence. I would argue that it gives us privilege in some cases and in some circles. The language is thus a cultural "double-edged sword"; it has two sides, of course a positive and a negative side. It is a cultural medium, with its inspiring imaginative nature giving rise to diversity of ideas. Let's unpack this, equity, in general (not just in fashion), needs to be present, because everyone has a unique lifespan and experience that shapes insights, ideas, intuitions; you name it! It can also be seen critically: sometimes enacting a division (let's go back to the term *privilege* for a second.) It can privilege people and create hierarchies, but we can be vigilant, self-aware, and collectivistic (to a healthy extent) to make strides in preventing a stratified or hierarchical structure.

  The other cultural concept here is *groups*. There are subcultures of fashion, but there are also fashion neighborhoods and spaces where fashion is pronounced and flourishes. To implement a sound approach to fashion, we need to actualize how important it is to be a global citizen. To be an active global citizen, we should have our minds open, like our worlds are open. We cannot think myopically, so we must consider all matters (in and out of fashion) wholly and holistically. To call upon Belle in *Beauty and the Beast*, there *is* more than this provincial life (Truesdale & Wise, 1991.) Go find it!

  We must learn to appreciation plurality and the multiplicity of ideas I referenced before. Regardless any factors that distinguish a person, ideas and insights are in everyone's arsenal. We should all employ and expend them, because we have brilliant ideas to offer to this world.

Fashion has fascinated me for as long as I can remember, so when someone dismisses it as trivial or frivolous, which, under my impression sadly does happen, it feels so incorrigibly wrong to me. When people are dismissive of fashion and the arts and stick to calling them such names and giving them such epithets, they are overlooking, maybe even ignoring, its monumentally beneficial, insightful, denoting, connoting, and favorable facets. These facets are as follows (this list is exhaustive at best):

1. Fashion's nonlinearity and its dynamic timeline, full of ins and outs and lessons;
2. Its cultural climate and histories that parallel society and culture and time;
3. Its resonances to a space or place in the world;
4. Fashion is interdisciplinary and intertextual, thus making it also interdependent. It is inextricably linked and attached to other disciplines of knowledge, insight, thought, etc. Its ideas are influenced and intertwined with other disciplines, and it has resonances and appearances in other mediums and "texts" that is can be "read", or interpreted with.
5. Its ability to mirror time and place and explicate it further, acting collectively as an anthology of anecdotes and information (partly from research);
6. Its revolutionary power to make change and act as a "guiding light" and a vehicle for change;
7. The fact that it has existed for eons but has evolved through time as well;
8. Lastly, I find it super ironic that we universally and commonly use fashion on a daily, very regular basis, and people can be so dismissive of its very self-evident and telling importance.

Introduction

Fashion demands more than one monolithic "truth." With a variety of perspectives on it that range from qualitative and positivist to quantitative yet philosophically rooted, fashion studies cohere transnationally, so the consumerism of fashion is one myriad people can relate to. Fashion and time arguably influence each other and exists as corollaries, intricately and suggestively. The question to ponder on is if they can keep up with each other.

Fashion is malleable and fits into many molds, that is why (as I referenced in the preface of this book) it is quite a demanding task to paint it as it is, a comprehensive and all-encompassing picture of the world and times. Fashion is ubiquitous and cathartic and therapeutic: it exists in myriad ways in the contexts it fills and is a medium of rejoicing and reinventing oneself. It is endlessly expressive and can be a useful outlet for anxieties. Especially now, in the COVID-19 era, the paradox that we all may need "retail therapy" or any therapy through clothes and fashion but cannot go anywhere so we consume (physically) less fashion and clothing at this time, is stark and conceivably hard to navigate. My solution is to continue to keep up with how the world is using fashion and keep ourselves sane by thinking forward. It is exceedingly difficult to propose a resolute, hard-wired solution to this when uncertainty is surrounding us all. Reconciling this paradox is a task that will need close consideration, but it is beneficial to acknowledge the existence of this paradox.

Fashion is semiotic, poetic, and multifaceted; it demands to be defined. It manifests itself in material forms and cultural contexts. Fashion is a relational medium of communication, whether one would think of it as communicative or not. It is approached as having personal ties and symbolic value (Crane and Bovone, 2006.) It is a material object of study and invites criticism as people think of it as trivial. At surface, it is artistic; it is aesthetic. One can veer deeply into clothing articles and trends and even examine concepts immanent to the field of fashion, like consumption.

In Bovone and Crane (2006), the article talks about nationalism and boundaries. I've always seen fashion as transcending languages and spaces, so this brings up that question. It also questions fashion's universalities and Benedict Anderson's "nationalism." The production and consumption are relevant to creating and fostering thought and communities... these point me to Anderson's "imagined communities." Face-to-face communication is key. It is being diminished by technology and relates to personal selling and retail. This can also be used to also talk about how technology is taking over communication. I have also studied how social media is disrupting innovation and imaginative thought in fashion and visionary thought. I remember being introduced to the term "technological determinism." It deals briefly with the presentation of fashion and its connotation, which has altered and evolved fickly over time. It has, assuredly yet subtly. We will delve into theories and theoretical framework(s) later in the book, but can ideas like the "digital divide" and "technological determinism" be looked at as theories? By the way, the digital divide is another timeless, universal, telling issue, like many issues in fashion; it is the discrepancy of access to technology between social classes or groups, while technological determinism is the determining or characterization and utilization of technology based on society

Fashion is lived; it is envisioned. We envision style, and we hopefully or ideally ideate it. We realize it and circulate it and are all creators of it through such a system. We live each other's vision. We all become inadvertently accustomed to this circular, cyclical system of exchange. We circumnavigate it routinely.

Fashion is thankfully a researchable medium, as many people seek to research it and tease out its intricacies, subtleties, and even its anxieties. Its dialectics become more self-evident and apparent through its studies, and it is inextricably intertwined with culture, communication, and mass media, as we will explore. It is researchable, but is it quantifiable? I know for a fact we can conduct studies both qualitatively and quantitatively, but this still begs the question of how. The insight the world vastly and conveniently provides us for this is key, as objects and culture reflect on this. Fashion's zeitgeist demonstrates theoretical foundations and creates temporal as well as geospatial and geopolitical boundaries and settings to supplement and guide research further in its field.

All of the issues in fashion can be debated, and that is where a push and pull of tensions and tumult occurs. Issues in fashion can range from frivolous to serious, in academia and people's perceptions; to me they are all important and incessantly fraught. Issues hotly debated include sustainability, consumerism, and public relations and marketing approaches to trend forecasting and analysis and artistic or aesthetic means of fashion.

Though fashion must be given attentive and meticulous care and consideration, sometimes critical, sometimes methodological, it does have unrestricted and free potential to stomp out problems and tease out anxieties, whether social or cultural or individual or institutionalized. Recently, we see a rise in activism and solidarity with the untimely, gruesome, and ineffably unruly death of Mr. George Floyd. We see the rise on social media of hashtags like #BlackLivesMatter and had a day dedicated to Black lives where users posted a black background to commemorate and elucidate violence inflicted upon the Black community. It is dire and evident that there is a crucial need to support Black-owned businesses. One of those is Rekless Creations, under the direction of Brittany Wongus. I interviewed her about her slogans and process behind her Revolution tee, which features the word time", very apparently inspired by *Time Magazine*. Then it signals Black solidarity, uprising, and power. The interview will appear later on in this book.

A highly visual medium, fashion is a platform that can be studied greatly and multidirectional-ly. The book will explore research methods I have learned, like ethnography and digital ethnography, interviewing (both qualitative and quantitative), polls and surveys, focus groups, and textual and content analysis. It will be concerned heavily with theories like Thorstein Veblen's emulation, Pierre Bourdieu's distinction, Thorstein Veblen's trickle-up and trickle-down theories, and fashion's theories of trickle-up and trickle-down and trickle-across. It will also delve into the hierarchy of needs by Abraham Maslow and other theories of mass communication, sociology, psychology, and anthropology.

Defining Fashion

Fashion is a process that is mediated. It is challenging to continue to decipher a definition for the expansive domain of fashion, but it can also be disputed that fashion has "no content" (Martinez & Bovone, 2012.) It is "ephemeral and elusive" and is a "target that keeps moving" (Agins, 1999.) The fashion world faces inevitable obsolescence, and an example is women's skirt lengths or the silhouette of men's widening and thinning trousers (Agins, 1999.)

Fashion is defined, by Phyllis G. Tortora and Sara B. Marcketti (2015), as a taste shared between myriads of people over a certain period of time. They go on to say that, socially, it extends beyond clothing, and to add, I would assert that food influences fashion, as well as nature and even machines like Tortora and Marcketti (pg. 9) say "autmobiles"; they cite furniture as well.

The argument to this is that it is indispensably artistic, which gives it aesthetic content. Also, the fact that innovators and designers promote and create fashion with an intent implies that fashion has meaning. It is a meaning-making process.

I want to propose fashion is a process of cultural consumption. I am sure I did not just coin a new direction of thought or a new term; I am sure sociologists have thought of this term and used it. It speaks to origins of style, and style is something, incidentally, that can be considered social-psychologically and endlessly sociologically and materially. Origins of style can trace back to socialization and social interaction. A sociological mode of thinking that can easily be attribute to style is sociology's "symbolic interactionism", coined by George Herbert Mead, who never published work on it. Fashion is endemic, as the garments are, to the owner. They are symbolic, and such symbolisms clash and interact to create unique agency and meaning. Through a curriculum, a "hidden curriculum" coined by Philip Jackson in 1968, socialization occurs. This could be through institutions like schools, daycares, or religious institutions, or disembodied, more abstract ideals like culture or religion itself. Dating and who we date is an example of influence on us. For example, did you know Madonna dated artists Jean-Michael Basquiat? This has to have had a bearing on her style, even if temporarily. I read this in Shahida Bari's 2020 book, *Dressed*. It is a cultural consumption along with capital, whether that capital is cultural, social, or symbolic capital; these "capitals" were proposed by Pierre Bourideu in his seminal social theories (1986.)

Fashion can be a social construct in both concrete and abstract senses. What I mean by this is that it is material and physical when describing the embodying and tangible products, whatever they may be, and corporeal as they compose a body of thought and of practice. The thought is consumerism and consumer behavior and philosophy, and the practice is the physical and physiological manifestations of fashion and its anatomy. It is disembodied when it is abstract. It is circulated and perpetuated, and this is also fashion and its lifespan. It is inevitable that it will trickle-down from media, as celebrities, influencers, movies, films, and popular culture place it at the forefront of the media itself and market it to mass populations and demographics. As a body situated and contextualized in time and space, it encompasses other sociologies and social constructs, which is extremely vital. It is a body that helps us make sense of the social climate and constructs like mores and folkways and cultures.

Fashion, as a social construct, is perpetuated colossally and fluidly. All kinds of people adopt fashion everyday and live it. As a social construct, it is the classifications that manifest themselves in society. Fashion is coherent with society and a form of rebelling against society and trends as well.

Fashion can be traces into literature and art. Two examples from art and literature are the red hat Holden Caulified gives to his younger sister, Phoebe, in J.D. Salinger's *Catcher in the Rye*, and spinning and textiles in mythology as per Norse mythology's Holda and Perchta or Greek mythology's Philomela, who used it to fight back against her rape and silencing (where he tongue was cut out); the design is still studied to this day (Motz, 1984.)

Fashion is historically grounded and notable; it indicates advances in technology and culture, and it demonstrates traditional and cultural rituals while also displaying "artistic imagination" (Wolfe, 2019.) Clothing satiates needs beyond being a basic necessity of humankind; these are physical or physiological, psychological, and social as well. Adornment, as psychological need, validates self-concepts and reaffirms beauty. Culture is defined myriad ways, but it pertains to socialization and values; it is universal but not everyone perceives cultures the same. Folk costumes enforce particular, ethnic beauty but people's ideas of beauty are not fixed. They waver over time (Wolfe, 2019.) Personality and individuality naturally seep into a person through fashion. Making people distinct from one another, and other traits like sociability and economic responsibility is indicative by fashion.

Fashion is inextricable to its prescient and telling intertwinings in media and academia, but that is extrinsic to the field itself. We can assuredly consider intersections in its elaborate intrinsic fields, like fashion marketing, fashion journalism, fashion in a broader sense (like arts or culture), etc. as these are all tied to each other indispensably and instrumentally. It is a predictive medium, where making the future (near and far) is not only a task of eliminating myopia and being far-sighted and ready, (which is underestimated increasingly), but when fashion makes the world foreseeable and makes the future conceivable, it is an intrinsic and congenital process. The projected ideas of the future come from all contexts, eras, places and spaces, disciplines, influences, fields, etc., and define the forthcoming and make it bearable upon the fashion world and cultural milieus.

This is usually and partly defined by trends and trend forecasting. "Trend", as a word, is holistically and entirely multilayered. We now see it manifest in life and the world of social media and mass media. We see *what is trending* to know what is current. Fashion forecasting is invaluable and vital. Of course, that is why it exists and is insurmountably important. It cannot even be stated how integral this role of the forecasters is to fashion and the artistic fashion world.

Trends go in and out; they are characteristically cyclical. They rivet us and make the world categorizable and ascertain a sensibility about culture, art, fashion, food, entertainment (music, television, film), academia, mass communication, etc. They are bound to us people. They are ubiquitously present and evergreen.

Fashion is usually deemed artistic, but there is also science to it. When these word in unison, fashion is conceptualized. It described is massively public and personal. It is often viewed through social and cultural shifts and economic conditions. The zeitgeist also measures when spirits and tensions are high; when spirits are high, there is a positive correlation with consumerism. People tend to dress in playful and liberal ways as opposed to being reserved when tensions are high and spirits are low. Dress standards can change with social structure, and these conditions affect one another conversely (Wolfe, 2019.) Dress standards work in tandem with social structures and influence consumerism. When considering consumerism and purchasing behaviors, needs and wants are requisite to be assessed.

Consumerism: Needs and Wants

In this discourse, needs rare measured as something necessary for survival—protection and livelihood. Wants are what arguably constitute consumerism. Assuredly, people do shop for necessities, but satisfaction, one of Maslow's basic needs in his hierarchy, should be satiated. Fashion consumers have both needs and wants for clothing, for example: warm coats for cold weather, and these both are imperative in consumption and society.

People shop for timeless classics and transient fads. A "sudden burst of popularity" with "floods of imitations" constitutes a fad (Wolfe, 2019.) Attributable by its ostentatious, excessive design, this is a trends that does not stay, as it fades with swiftness. A fad can also cause hype, buzz, craze, or mania, essentially encouraging people to exchange communication about it by wearing it and internalizing it or perpetuating it. A fad can become a "style" due to its virality, or if its conception is viable.

Classics are long-standing, enduring trends that can resist change and evolution in fashion. Being sought-after, they can be updated but are evergreen styles. The simplistic appeal and stylish lines of these garments is what gives them appeal and protects them from becoming out-of-date (Wolfe, 2019.)

Consumers ultimately determine what is in vogue or not. Only consumers can dictate the field and what they want to wear (Wolfe, 2019.) There is much multifaceted communication with this, but consumers nonverbally communicating their desire for a fashion or not by not consuming the fashion. Price is not a determining factor for fashionableness of a garment. Ideas conceived at virtually any price level are eventually copied in budgets that cater to everyone. Fashions can be perpetuated through mass and visual communication and promotional activities do not affect viability of a fashion; however, they do encourage but cannot impose it. Promotion of fashion does not strengthen a trend and neither can it revive a trend that is fading away (Wolfe, 2019.) The designers and manufacturers are not powerless, but the cycle of fashion has made the market of fashion a consumer-driven terrain. Shedding a light on designers provides a contextual and telling background to approach this domain with. Next, the book will assess Giorgio Armani.

The Case of Armani

Knockoffs agitated Giorgio Armani, as they were a source of validation for those below who imitated him. His unconstructed suit was mimicked, so he would not retain this mark of his originality. This obviously irked him, as did press and mass media. *Miami Vice* style became characteristic to Giorgio Armani, as it propagated his clothes, and viewers even tuned in to it for the sole purpose of seeing these clothes. This is essentially the might embedded in clothing and its intertextuality with media and consumption. The pleated pants and unconstructed blazers worn in *Miami Vice* were canonized to Armani and amplified consumerism, as people shopped. Armani stated men do not need to look a certain way; men did not need to look overstated or gaudy. His approach to "menswear" was never "fashion", as he said (Agins, 1999.) Consuming Armani's designs or anyone's innovative designs is consumer culture, which is intertwined with the physical and mobile spaces in which they consume.

Space, Context, and Merchandising

In her book, *The End of Fashion*, Teri Agins argues (1999) that there has been a dramatic shift in how stores are perceived and display merchandise. Department stores used to be eccentric, exhilarating places with wondrous displays. They used to, incidentally, be places where one can reflect on aesthetic appeal and farsighted, inventive designers and innovative minds. Now, they invoke drollness and are essentially dull (Agins, 1999.)

The reputation of department stores has wavered drastically, as they used to be epitomes of excitement and newness. They used to shed light on and feature the exotic and glitzy ideals and items and appeal that consumers so eagerly coveted. In today's economic milieu, as Agins argues (1999), department stores have become "predictable." The stores echo constraint, as they are cautious and appeal to their own profit, when many argue this is a consumer-driven economy. That is debatable and not ubiquitously applicable, but using a profit-driven approach in an economy rendered and decided by those who shop is not an avenue advisable to be taken. This is because it would simply not fit. It would contradict the dogmatic, paradigmatic shift that the context has taken. Department stores created a camaraderie with populaces in the past, delivering style in widespread ways to larger cities. Agins cites Neiman Marcus as a notable store, and later Bloomingdales. These made designers recognizable, like even novel, fresh designers like Ralph Lauren who introduced the necktie and Yves Saint Laurent (Agins, 1999.) Bloomingdale's, shortened as "Bloomies" was regarded as the "retailing theater" and offered experiences as well as accessibility for high-fashion and commemorative memorabilia, like themed bags (Agins, 1999.)

Competition was a motivator as well as menacing to fading retailers like Marshall Fields. Nordstrom easily saw an opportunity to take over and assert its newfound presence in the market. With a slogan like "Our buyers are your neighbors", Nordstrom started to win hearts of consumers and the culture of shopping. The market shifted as retailers recognized a uniformity in buyers' attitudes toward fashion. What someone in one city would desire to buy, another person in another city would want also. The same merchandise was stocked in all stores, and there was am evident practicality in this. Buyers, thus, temporarily were disconnected with the market, as they could not control what they bought. Image and perception became enormously important in the fashion world. Women started to choose Gap because of its enticing image and prices. It was successful behind Levi's with its other sects like Banana Republic and Old Navy. It was a fashion destination that offered affordability, authenticity, yet newness (Agins, 1999.) This begs a question: is Gap's unassuming, genuine stance on clothing that evokes realness and authenticity against fashion? According to Agins, Gap did not rebel against fashion and rather pronounced the individuality behind a fashion's wearer (1999.) It created its own stylish movements in fashion, redefining fashion and itself (Agins, 1999.)

This could possibly bring into the critical conversation and necessitate and beg the question of the existence and corporeality of the "cyborg body" that Susan L. Foster cites in *Coreographing Empathy* (2011.) She considers the critically facilitated interface between humankind and technology, namely the cell phone's GPS (global positioning system.) Some cannot go anywhere without it; trust me! I had a friend who had been to my house thousands of times a few years ago, and every single time he'd lose direction and need the GPS. Not only him but innumerable, colossally many people have deemed and rendered this technology indispensable to life and even to their "selves." The "cyborg" body is made up of this technology that tracks us. Our accessories (namely technological accessories) are more pronounced and seemingly more prominent than our fashion accessories, hypothetically speaking. I would not agree with this statement. When I wear my bracelets (I am obsessed with bracelets; they usually complement my summer outfits) I usually make them stand out as statements and not mere additions or emblazonments. I want eyes to be on them and to be drawn to them. Do our fashion accessories render us "fashion-cyborgs?" I would not imagine they have the same readily deleterious, precocious effects that cellular phones and technology in general have on us, but could they possibly? Could be become self-defeatingly, immobilizing-ly, paralyzed and dependent upon fashion accessories? These questions are transient and almost non-existent, as no one pays attention to them... They are just really arbitrary, aren't they? Or are they? Do they matter? It is still something we can inadvertently fall into; thus, we may consider such questions from time to time.

As is prominently and naturally obvious, fashion and its study does not exist in a vacuum. Since I have stated this cliché, to make it more elucidated and less trite, I will reiterate that countless (even unnamable) factors meld to shape and mold the malleable and open fields and realms of fashion. Rocamora and Smelik (2015) refer to the "presumed temporal sequence and geographical inscription" (p. 7) of a fashion that is perhaps inevitably and unavoidably modernizing and globalizing. The chronological sequence and geographical locations of this fashion are infinite and possibly even undefinable. Fashion exists everywhere, ubiquitously, and as such, is inscribed and embossed into the terrains and domains it penetrates. Ascription to fashion, then, is highly unavoidable. Fashion is fundamentally unavoidable as it is. Fashion inhabits spaces and inspires desire, as is suggested by Louise Crewe (2017) in *Geographies of Fashion*. There is an axiomatic and apparent "push and pull" in the social and cultural landscape of fashion. This is another point that materialize the fact that fashion, once again, does not **exist in a vacuum**.

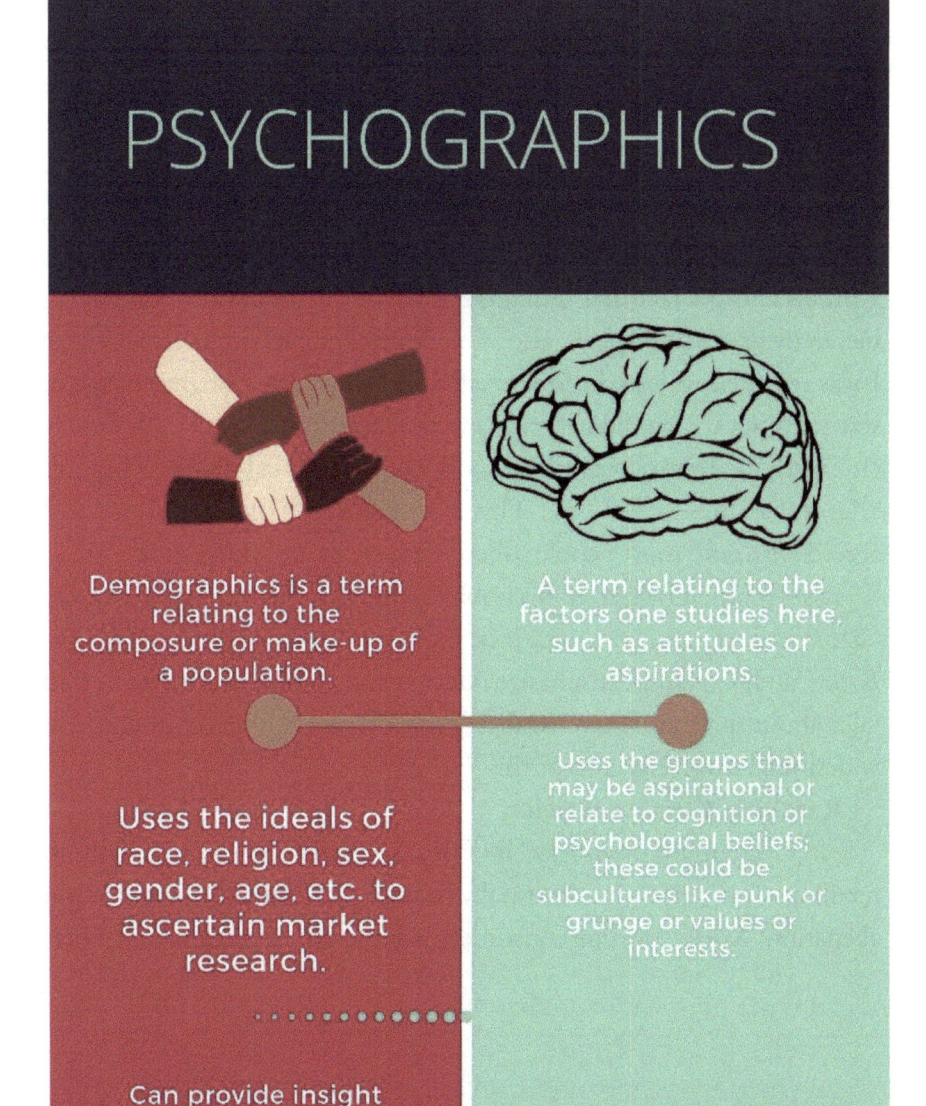

INTRODUCTION — | 13 |

DEMOGRAPHICS

V S

PSYCHOGRAPHICS

Demographics is a term relating to the composure or make-up of a population.

A term relating to the factors one studies here, such as attitudes or aspirations.

Uses the ideals of race, religion, sex, gender, age, etc. to ascertain market research.

Uses the groups that may be aspirational or relate to cognition or psychological beliefs; these could be subcultures like punk or grunge or values or interests.

Can provide insight into what racial or

It can intuitively

Brick-and-mortar retailing stands against TV-retailing and e-tailing which is digital and intensely mobile (Wolfe, 2019.) Personal selling, which is highly personable, includes going door-to-door. Thrift stores are specialized and more temporary notions and forms of retailing, like pop-up shops, exist. Dynamic retailing avenues are constantly being instilled and evolving (Wolfe, 2019.)

The point where Jonah Berger mentions colors as labels or indicators that constitute a system, or the point where he mentions how Burberry posts its customers' photos to an online montage, can also offer ideas to take from the novel. The reader can see how Burberry is cited as being enormously concerned with its customers and consumers, such that it includes them in its own advertising and engaging experiences; note however, they are not the only company to do this in the fashion business, as the online fashion marketplace, ASOS.com, also involves its customers in its photos, wearing the clothes they bought from ASOS.com, in #AsSeenOnMe. The novel reiterates prevalent social ideas, like status symbols and the fact that humans engage in the tradition of displaying hierarchy or status displays, also. This is another part of the novel where I was tempted to look inside myself and think how I might engage in status displays. Also, Berger reiterates that art, music, beauty, (definitely also aesthetic beauty), and transcendence of spiritual or other boundaries, cause one to feel awe. This is something I thought about and agreed with, and most people subconsciously do not think of it.

Lasltly, Jonah Berger, in his book *Contagious: How Things Catch On* (2013) and Al Reis along with Jack Trout in 1980 book *Positioning: The Battle for Your Mind*, emphasize internet and virality. Since this section talks about space and merchandising the internet exhibits countless and widespread manifestations of this.

Retailing Communication

There are varying levels of business communication in fashion retailing. Customers should usually be approach with less pressure and alienation. Satisfaction of consumers is indicative of customer service.

Customer service has to be heavily institutionalized and practiced on all levels of the organization. Service quality has to be practiced in approach and customer expectations. This is defined as how well the services are executed to consumers (Wolfe, 2019.)

Price positioning and value positioning must be conducted on all levels of retailing. Mostly employed by discount stores for more mass circulated items, price positioning allows customers to compare and contrast items of interest. Kohl's practices value positioning, where price is fixed at a middle-price-point (Wolfe, 2019.)

Making customers feel as if they should not regret purchases is defined as reinforcement. Assuring the customer to feel good is also making them feel good about the purchase, which may have been impulsive or risky. Following up with a customer is also crucially important; proactive and reactive communication is key. A multilateral communication between consumer and retailer creates clientele that are loyal. Responding and not being impersonal are recommended to keep customer loyalty and incentivizing consumption (Wolfe, 2019.) This creates the necessity to question the resistance to a consumerism that is duping and victimizing societies. A subtle, yet conversational approach and greeting is advised when bonding, creating meaningful and lasting relationships with consumers, patrons, and customers, occurs. Consumers are also classified as *casual lookers*, who are more casually interested in seeing what kind of merchandise is available. These casual lookers should be left alone after being given a friendly greeting; this will incentivize them to return. *Undecided customers* need to be dealt with, with patience. They will analyze garments' care properties and prints and evaluate them. *Decided customers* are resolute and should be dealt with effectively and cautiously. They already have made their decision, so superfluous conversation can aggravate them (Wolfe, 2019.)

Place is important and is essential to fashion marketing, even marketing in general. A store can be located in a business district or a neighborhood shopping center; this is overlooked but highly impactful. Market coverage is important with place. Place, like all other marketing strategies, must be succinct and fiercely microtargeted. It is important to consider internal place, like the design of the store, as well as external place like location. Differentiating oneself from competitors and grounding its image is very imperative as well, as retailers keep an image and reputation and have large duties. Representing and ascertaining a consistent and enticing image is major, as well as delving into the buyer's motives (Wolfe, 2019.) Fashion cities, as coined in 2009 by Agnes Rocamora, like New York City and Milan are where market weeks and trade shows are held. These are where more rampant and forceful consumerism takes place. Los Angeles is also a fashion city with myriad visionaries, but New York is further recognized as a "fashion city" because of its geographic location and accessibility. I remember living in Northridge, as I was attending my graduate program, and I did a project concerning the garment factories and the Calle Jones in downtown Los Angeles.

. In communication, theorizing space is made even more convenient by the term, territory (Adler, Proctor II, & Rosenfeld, 2010.) I learned it as haptics. I added this in here because social-scientifically, space is imperative. Social science takes theoretical approaches and can explain fashion. The spaces we inhabit in a certain outfit are not fixed. They are wavering and flexible.

After discussing some designers and their case studies along with topics that can potentially be researched in fashion, I want to say this section may seem like a hodgepodge and as helplessly arbitrary, but let's make sure that is not the case. This section should have set things up, even though it is very specific and detailed. It should also be equally enlightening and not just supplemental or anecdotal.

Conclusion

My vision for this book is a promising one. I want the target audience to be everyone, but of course this is not a leisurely book to be read by everyone. I want to cater to everyone, because as I have always argued, fashion is an innate process and discipline that we indispensably participate in—all of us. I will seek to cater to everyone, and assuredly that is my aim and intention, so this can be read as a philosophical text. I seek to emulate a seminal text and a telling text of epiphanies and revelations, but not to digress further, I want to not be exceptional or exclusive. To put it quite simply, this is a book for anyone, but especially for minds that gravitate toward art, culture, and fashion. This is not a textbook but is not restricted so that it cannot be used so.

Intertwining social media, mass media, word-of-mouth, intercultural, interpersonal, and intergender communication, journalism, social science, behavioral science, marketing and consumer behavior, etc., with research, pedagogies, epistemologies, and methodologies, with book will hopefully prove to be an embodiment and disembodiment of voice and space of all kinds. Although it uses my voice, it will draw from voices and key thinkers and theorists and grounded, common knowledge to illustrate dialogue fostered by research in the discipline of fashion.

In this developing age of "hyperdigitalism"—the tendency and zeal of virtually everyone to engage with social, mass, and increasingly technological media—this book considers settings that are physical (concrete) and abstract. It considers, extensively, the settings that constitute fashion and culture and where this all can be cultivated, grown, enhanced, dialogued, seen (in multisensory manners), heard, viewed critically, conceived or perceived, or enriched.

Fashion can be complicit in perpetuating presumptive and indiscreet ideas and concepts. One can favor fashion it its entirely while seeing critical avenues to approach it. In fact, this is eminent and immanent. A motivated field, fashion is innately personified and personable. A peripatetic artform, it exists in all cultures but can still epitomize (however innocuously) cultural appropriation. This is not to be taken lightly, as some depictions of race, ethnicity, culture, or ideology can be inherently misguided or misinformed and flawed; these can be extremely offensive.

When you are researching or investigating fashion, you are uncovering complex, ingrained, and universal truths. The ubiquity and uncertainty of fashion's character supplements the study. You are not only researching its subtleties and intricacies, but you are digging into its essence and intrinsic DNA. You are delving uniquely deeply into axiomatic, empirical, pressing questions; this is equally intriguing and riveting. You are using a critical and methodological lens to approach it, rather than a purely aesthetic lens. You are eliminating and preventing bias and triviality and not letting things seem trite. In fashion is embedded an intractably cyclical world, one that changes incessantly and profusely poses news and reinvents, recontextualizes, and redefines ideas, settings, concepts, arts, aesthetics, philosophies, and globalities and eliminates redundancies and monotonies. It is quite enlivening and enriching to certify, market, and ascertain fashion markets and fashion trends. It is vital and essential (more than we realize) to be increasingly inquisitive, pensive, methodical, observant, perceptive of, and receptive to fashion.

Just a disclaimer and overdone reminder: correlation and causation are not implied by each other. Cause and effect is a telling scenario as well as correlation, and it is rewarding and important to pay close attention to such phenomena. For example, wearing beach clothes or summer clothes must very likely correlate to ice cream consumption, because they both happen when it is hot. I make this relation (correlation) because I remember in a psychology class in community college, the professor was explaining correlation and used the example that people get ice cream when they are angry: i.e.—they correlate. Why? The correlate because they both happen when the weather is hot.

One thing I would like to include incidentally is how fashion has material and immaterial artefacts and angles. It is both concrete and abstract.

Intertextualities of Fashion: Literature and Onwards

Fashion is hyperbole at best and verisimilitude at its undesirable points. It is both because it embodies the hyperreal and surreal and makes the idealistic appear realistic. Anything can be synecdochic of fashion, because virtually anything can add up to it and be defined by it. For example, many ideals are part of fashion—and fashion can be treated as the whole. We can use apostrophe to make odes to fashion—as apostrophe is used when we call inanimate or abstract things. Fashion is abstract and intangible, but it is also material and physiological—so in that domain we can debate: is it ever even inanimate? Fashion embellishes mundanity, turning in into modernity. It is definitely not inanimate and is typically multidimensional (from any angle.)

We can make allusions with fashion—this is intrinsic to its cyclical nature. The trends—the ins and outs and ups and downs of fashion—the subcultures—are alluded to time and time again. We make allusions as researchers, observers, designers, students of the art, etc. We refer to the old—and the new is reminiscent of the old, quite immutably and indispensably.

Fashion also engages in objectification. This should never be conflated with an idea that fashion is principally objective, where it is not. It is subjective and can definitely be approached and looked at with an objective, more partial lens. It is highly subjective and variable, but one can fixate, situate, and contextualize it in order to assess it with an objective perspective. Let's go back to how it engages in objectification—objectification, is by definition, a literary device. It is when an author (in this case as visionary or innovator) takes an abstract ideal and makes it embodied or tangible. Fashion's innovators or researchers can do this by taking ideas and ideologies and materializing or amplifying them on a garment. It may not become strictly physical, keeping elements of the sublime, but it is material, undoubtedly.

When we talk about objectification, it is simply tempting to talk about how men and women are objectified in advertising, but we also see that the phrase, "I shop; therefore I am", is more evident and eminent as time goes on. Are we dupes of fashion then? We need to be watchful and cautious of this. Fashion can hold us captive! This is seldom unhealthy for us—but we cannot let it dictate us. Fashion can define us and it CAN dictate us.

Fashion can be soliloquy—a heard or unheard monologue. In being a soliloquy, it expresses concealed and undisclosed thoughts in a way where it does not need to consider being heard or unheard. Some of the soliloquy can be intrinsic and internal. It can be retrospective and reflective, as it as an art—it is also restorative. It can remind us of our mistakes (not repeated or bad outfits.) It can remind us of overconsumption, being ostentatious, being irresponsible, or being indolent or oblivious to fashion's trends and implications. It speaks of these in volumes out loud. It amplifies the monologue or soliloquy—reminiscent sometimes of an eerily almost Shakespearean style and art.

There are myriad ways in which fashion metaphorizes life. It is remarkably a metaphor for life's experiences, trials, triumphs, celebrations, and tribulations. It acts very recognizably as a mirror, and I am not talking about it being a reflection of the self but of times and lifespans. What comes to mind is first how fashion's ebbs and flows mirror the coherence of life and its disruptions too. Of course, this is consistent with the idea that fashion is a mirror or reflection of social and cultural times and trends.

I am tempted to talk about textiles as metaphors. There are so many traits of a textile that can be allegorical or metaphoric. They can tell stories and be reflective of us, from a micro to macro level. Their appeal in this regard ranges. We can talk about momie, and how it is unbalanced and gives off a haphazard or wayward feel. Wouldn't it be awesome if this became colloquial or universal? We could say "you're being really momie today" when someone is scatterbrained, even indecisive.

We can refer to someone as resilient or resistant. Textiles can be abrasion and water resistant (Kadolph, 2010.) To me, abrasion resistance mirrors inability to be torn or worn, so it would be a mentally and physically strong person. Resilience just takes this a few steps further, pointing to how someone bounces back or recovers from being molded or affected. To me, this could refer to moods and how fast someone processes emotion or how well they understand their emotions. This could mean, in the physiological realm, someone bouncing back from any kind of injury, being intense or severe. Someone can be porous or absorbent with knowledge or with moods. They can take in the moods or the energies surrounding them and become grouchy or radiate positivity. Porous personalities would be infectious—invigorating and enlivening people around them.

FASHION: Aspects, Processes, Thoughts, Methods

Before we get into the study of fashion – I want to bring up one term: diagnosticity. To me this is a term that relates to how measurable a theme in fashion is. It dictates the duration of studying the item at hand and the intensity, or how devoted the examiner is to a certain item of observation or examination. It consists of three impacting factors: propensity, plausibility, and consistency.

This is the **researcher's** behavior and inclination to document a certain way. This is important because they (the researcher) cannot let biases or judgements cloud their research. They have to remain impartial, focused, and objective. They need to collect information but at the same time be wary of their propensities.

Plausibility is how realistic the researcher is. Fashion can feel dreamy and, but it is up to us to keep our research grounded and relatable. Studying fashion is arguably mostly conceptual, but it can be concretized when reported.

We need to focus on consistency of how we study fashion. We cannot go back-and-forth and diminish our focus. We can gain influence from primary, secondary, global, and historical sources, but we have to remain constant. What needs to remain constant is our focus. Shifting our attention to another cause has the effect of depletion.

We also need to keep a focal point. We need to realize that fashion is not only global and ubiquitous in its reach, but that it is practiced by virtually everyone; that is why Farnan and Stone (2023), say that "everyone is in on it" (pg. 5.)

Fashion has a historical and worldly imprint. It is virtually irrevocable, which enables us to study its origins and influences today. It has been around like other arts and has a rich history. It goes from Ancient Egypt and Rome, to Baroque and Rococo to the Jazz Age, and from revolutions to utility (Franklin, 2019.)

Fashion, even if it is impermanent and ephemeral, immortalizes itself in many ways, roadmaps, instances, and its manifests itself into domains and terrains of all sorts on various levels. It manifests itself on runways, digital fashion week (because of COVID-19), fashion weeks, streets (where photography occurs), and parties (where a marketplace of ideas is embodied, as people dialogue at parties and immortalize the party itself and outfits in photographs.)

According to Bovone and Crane (2006), there are five approaches to studying fashion; most of these directly go to symbolic values and material culture. Consumption, which is also a focus of this reading, is something that connects with material culture, as I feel. I appreciated how it talked about constructing identity and realities and socialization. I also have read before (profusely) that the internet has made fashion more democratized and accessible; the article talks about democratization.

Bovone and Crane (2006) also talk about nationalism and boundaries. I've always seen fashion as transcending languages and spaces, so this brings up that question. It also questions fashion's universalities and Benedict Anderson's "nationalism." The production and consumption are relevant to creating and fostering thought and communities... these point me to Anderson's "imagined communities."

Another self-evident concept Bovone and Crane (2006) address and point to is that face-to-face communication is key. It is being diminished by technology and relates to personal selling and retail. I can use this to also talk about how technology is taking over communication. I have also studied how social media is disrupting innovation and imaginative thought in fashion and visionary thought. I remember being introduced to the term "technological determinism."

The endlessly amusing thing about fashion is that it can be examined, explored, delved into, investigated, etc.; the possibilities are non-exhaustive! Fashion can be so many "things" and things in general. It can be treated as so many things as well. Studied or taken at any times as an abstract idea, ubiquitous and intangible, and always (arguably always) as a material object or even a material phenomenon (stringed together by endless material objects), fashion poses boundlessly many questions and intimations and connections. Perhaps that is why I am able to evidently connect several, even numerous, research methods to the field. It becomes increasingly and exponentially more intriguing as we unpack its layers.

Fashion is a diversified, multilayered, multidimension realm and field that should be approached with a circumspect and open-minded approach. There are countless mediums of fashion, not just numerous. There are tremendously freighted with information and myths to debunk and unpack. They are thoroughly investigative as well. Whether we consider social media platforms or mass media in general, we still do not encompass all mediums. We also have irrevocably vivid and visual mediums and also more technical aspects of fashion, like production of it and processes of it. All of the "mediums" of fashion are indispensably creative. Television, movies, music, other film, and runway shows are exhibitive and visual. Illustrations and art direction are artistic and visual also, but just as, if not more innovative and creative. These all have answers engrained in them. When looking for answers to our questions about aesthetics of philosophy in fashion, there are all a convenient and telling starting point for us.

Giving a critical, methodological lens (that exists but is not recognized often as it should be recognized) can be revealing to the researcher, and fashion begs to be documented by people as well. It is authentic and reciprocal because it is self-evident, visual, inspirational, and aspirational. Ideas and ideals are "bounced off" of one another, and even if it is self-evident as "what you see is what you get", fashion is also much more than that, especially in a methodology and research.

Of course, crafting actionable, operational, and researchable research questions is extremely important. The following is an example of the research questions in a preliminary, rough form. The research questions should not connect only faintly or seem arbitrary to each other. They should serve to complement reach other and not seem uninformed.

RQs – Fashion/ Consumption

1. How do consumption habits become a consumer's identity or sense of being?
2. How do consumption habits predict future cultural and economic conditions?
3. In what ways is everyday communication complicit in creating desire?

These can serve to fill gaps in research and build bridges between mass communication, economics, and fashion consumerism.

What is a theory? How is it used/ implemented/ applied?

A theory can be intangible and abstract or concrete and tangible in its use. Its use can take two forms: practical (tactile, physical) and abstract (notional, explanatory.) Theories interrelate and carry sensibilities; they link together and explain and make sense of the issue or field at hand. According to Yuniya Kawamura (2020), theories are difficult to grasp and difficult to grasp and comprehend. Since they are manifest widely and do not surface physical. Arguably, they can be hard to study unless you make connections to something tangible. Theories are fluid, as they can be tangible, but arguably they cannot be this way at first. Theories are explaining the world and visionary ways and avenues to navigate thought. In their physical manifestations, they can be exemplified as objects of study that, as I would say, make a statement. That's right. These inanimate objects can very well be argumentative rather than static and only aesthetic in nature.

Theories can be imposing, menacing, and daunting. They aid us making and creating generalizations. They help us to create order in a disorderly, raucous, chaotic world. Theories thrive systematically and define and demand various methods. They inform methods and visa-versa (Kawamura, 2020.)

For example: four methods Kawamura outlines in "Doing Research in Fashion and Dress" are ethnography, survey methods, semiology, and object-based research. "The first two are obtrusive and the last two are unobtrusive measures" (Kawamura, 2020, pg. 25.) Theories help us to investigate and "establish relationships" (Kawamura, 2020.)

How can a theory add substance or direction to a study?

Theories are also referred to as theoretical frameworks. They can "frame the topic area and the method that you use" (Brennen, 2013, pg. 21.)

Theories are somewhat requisite and foundational to a study. They inform the entire study and are used repeatedly in different fields. In fashion, theories can be abstract, as previously mentioned, like abjectness or intentions, or they can be physical, like sunglasses or a t-shirt. Theories make us perceptive and are essentially ingrained in us. They inspire thought and are tied to theoretical orientations, as Kawamura (2020) calls them, and can tie to "functionalism" or "symbolic interactionism" (Kawamura, 2020, pg. 23.)

As Heike Jenss (2016) exemplifies through Martin Margiela's collections in his anthology, sources to study fashion are abundant. "Garments, photographs, exhibitions, catalogs, press releases, and lookbooks" (Jenns, 2016, pg. 154) are sources you can employ that offer inspiration and apsirations. Margiela exemplified the "ironization of nostalgia" in his Rotterdam Exhibition (Jenss, 2016, pg. 154.)

Theory and Practice

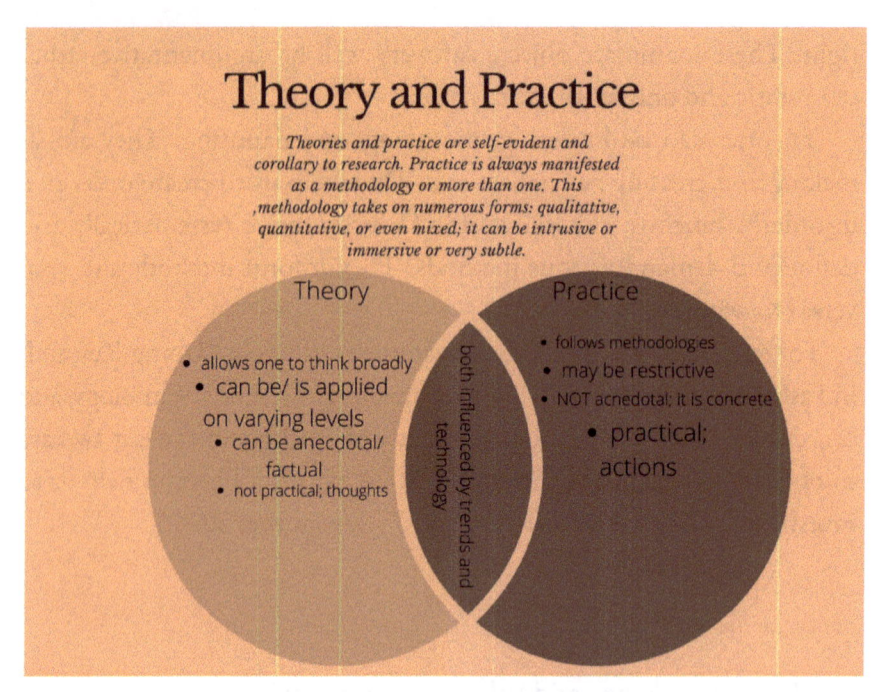

Theories and practice are self-evident and corollary to research. Practice is always manifested as a methodology or more than one. This ,methodology takes on numerous forms: qualitative, quantitative, or even mixed; it can be intrusive or immersive or very subtle.

Theory
- allows one to think broadly
- can be/ is applied on varying levels
- can be anecdotal/ factual
- not practical; thoughts

both influenced by trends and technology

Practice
- follows methodologies
- may be restrictive
- NOT acnedotal; it is concrete
- practical; actions

Theory and Practice Venn Diagram
Created by Umar Siddiqui on Canva.com

2 Infographic created on Canva.com, by Umar Siddiqui

What elements impact theories' livelihoods and "lifespans" and use?

There are numerous ideals and concepts that affect theories. There can be arborescent in the fact that some are more evident and eminent and some are less. Some have a more targeted effect on theories as some have a less didactic and striking effect on them.

The factors are (but are not limited to):

- Economics:

I am so terrible with economics, and as such, I have no mind to delve to deep into it. I managed to escape the course in all of my schooling up until now, when I am undergoing a fashion merchandising program. Fashion obviously and axiomatically intrigues me, and economics is inherent in *merchandising*, so (to add use of an economic term), this is a trade-off for me.

Typically, when I think of economics, I think of consumer behavior and consumerism. I think of market segmentation (which is basically just studying markets in a more structured way by separating and organizing them by interests and values, psychographics, and age and education.) I think of that more because I have taken a marketing course in undergraduate study. Anyway, with the way consumers interact with sales personnel, there is all kinds of customer service. I learned that there is **reactive** and **proactive** customer service. In reactive customer service, one handles customers' complaints and proactive customer service takes it a step further by evaluating customers' longings and desires (Wolfe, 2019.)

According to Mary G. Wolfe in 2019, baby boomers are retaining money and living longer lives, in turn remaining consumers. Millenials "enjoy personalization" and "want top design and quality at low prices" (pg. 558.) Zoomers, or Generation Z, thrive and strive for their own self-image, social media, and desire an experience they cannot forget.

- Politics and political climate

It is no secret or doubt that politics is in flux and affects fashion and theory. Theories apply to a wavering, fluctuating world of fashion of ins-and-outs, and politics applies to theory in the same way. Theory depends in political climate. Here, I do not mean republican, libertarian, independent, or democrat. Here, I am suggesting it applies a lot more generally, with movements that appeal to mass people but still have a highly political tinge to them, like minimum wage, or living wage, or immigration. These may not seem like they directly affect theory, but I can assuredly attest to that fact that they do. Immigration has been typically presented, in the United States, as a dichotomous, polarizing issue, when it is about people and affects more than just that realm of thought. It affects it by lending its tense battlefield of differing, dueling thought. Theory takes this as political climate and is shaped thusly. The minimum wage is something we usually hear needs to be a living wage. While I wholeheartedly agree, it also contributes to the political climate. The way things are at our borders and low-income homes cause us to be active and proactive and contribute to thought at large, in turn affecting and shaping theory.

- Psychological climate (internal and external)

I have an expansively tough time distinguishing between social factors and psychological factors, but that is not a warning. I will do my utmost and level best to describe this section accurately and adequately. Self-image and self-efficacy are intrinsic, and the outer factors like people's perceptions are the extrinsic part of this. Of course, image and efficacy are growing with the immutable rise of social media and (not to mention) narcissism. Psyche is affected by these factors and others and thus our cognition is affected. Words like these contribute to the ideas and outlook on theories and of theories.

- Trends (this is repetitive because trends occur and recur in everything)

This would be redundant, so let us say trends and developments are ubiquitous and that there are economic, social, cultural, political, and cognitive trends that affect theory.

- Technology

In this list, I have touched on social media, but digitalization and digital marketing projected as the future is something that is prescient, predictive, and telling. Social media has enable so many to establish so much with its evergreen and seemingly immortal legacy. The fact that theories are born out of this in such an exponential way and even an entrepreneurial way also suggests the mere opposite. Face-to-face communication is presently and direly diminishing, and this concerns thinkers as it suggests it is becoming obdurate, maybe even obsolete; theories are invariably coming out of this realm of thought.

- Culture and society

Culture is universal as a concept; it is ever-present and omnipresent. It is everywhere, but it differs everywhere it is. Society adopts culture, where culture dictates mores, folkways, norms, actions, beliefs, values, and attitudes (this is not exhaustive.) This begs me to be inquisitive. I want to ask: *is culture monolithic? Does it change?*

Surprisingly, that has not been mused in my experience so much. I have seen it not waver, and when it does, it takes on fluidity. It takes on a new, novel form. Anyway, it affects theory by being the backdrop of the theory, first and foremost. It also shapes it by adding or subtracting facets or forms of thinking about theory and humanity.

- Relational ideals

Relational ideals, like beauty, seem to be adopted mainly from the environment (be that media or word-of-mouth.) Relation ideals dictate how we perceive, and that is very revealing and influential for theory. Theory takes into account these ideals and can show them, as they seep into theory. Their interplay also can seep deep into theory.

- Communication climates

I would start by asserting that communication climates are heavily influenced and dictated by relational dialectics and ideals. We can examine relationships and how we communicate. While there are various factors affecting communication climates, the climates affect theory by, once again, being the ultimate backdrop, setting, and, yes, climate of the theory. These climates affect the atmosphere in which the theory in conceived and proposed. These climates ultimately make the theory fit for certain climates and settings while making the theory reject other settings.

And

- Linguistic settings

Language will likely echo communication and culture. It will create what I want to term "microcultures", which is most probably already coined. These, in my definition and worldview, are diasporic cultures but can also exist in a language of the native country or country of origin.

What are some theories commonly used to approach the field of fashion and its various subfields (aesthetics, philosophy, marketing, consumerism, etc.)?

CULTURE INDUSTRY- Theodor Adorno & Max Horkheimer -This interrelates to many theories we are discussing here. Adorno and Horkheimer suggest that enlightenment is deceiving us and we are duped through media (Adorno & Rabinbach, 1975.) Media, film and television, popular culture, etc. easily dictates fashions we wear and want to wear. It creates voids in our lives (looking from a critical lens) and apertures to fill. We need desire to keep us going and longing as well. That is how this theory relates to fashion.

CONSPICUOUS CONSUMPTION – Thorstein Veblen - Conspicuous consumption, in my humble opinion, deals with pretense and image-making. It is buying expensive or seemingly unattainable items rather than rudimental necessities. An example (in fashion) is buying the $375 Saint Laurent tee or extravagant jewelry.

According to Jenns (2016), fashion can ascertain identity and allow for escapism. As Kawamura (2018) says in *Fashion-ology*, production and consumption are corollaries to each other. She goes on to suggest that meaning-making is made through research and theory blending in realms of fashion. Consumerism is one of these realms; other than consumer behavior and that dialectic, it reveals so much. Distinction is made more apparent, and Bourdieu's notion and theory of Distinction is one to keep an eye on in this conversation.

NETWORKED COMMUNICATION – Manuel Castells – I would first like at assert that this might apply mostly when studied fashion media or fashion in media. The distinction is that there are media of fashion, like fashion magazines (GQ, Vogue) and podcasts and films (Nick Knight of SHOWStudio or other ventures like Phantom Thread (2017) and Personal Shopper (2016), or then fashion shows. On the other hand, there is fashion in media, so its use in popular culture like Disney costuming or costumes used in American Horror Story and its many seasons.

Castells saw expressive networks as coded by culture (2004.) He also said the "network society" is made up of "microelectronics-based information" and communication technologies" (pg. 3) Now, to relate this back to fashion, the increasingly, frankly inescapably technologized and networked terrain we regularly navigate has certainly made communication and consumerism in fashion easier. The fashions of the day (the reflections of the times) are captured and documented by technology, when before, (like dating back to very ancient times) documentation was through cave paintings where fashion and animal skins were depicted (Tortora & Marcketti, 2015.) Continuing through time, art, architecture, and fashion itself were a few of the physical yet also intangible facets of life that gave clues to times and fashion. Technology and innovation continued to grow. We know fashion has existed since humanity needed it for rudimentary things, like covering up or protecting oneself, and trade (with routes like the Silk Road, etc.) has existed too. We can resolutely say consumerism has existed influentially and archaically, but it has evolved, especially into networked consumerism; it has become more systematic, proactive, interactive, and intricate. Face-to-face communication is dwindling as we speak, especially with the prevalence of Zoom calls these days (in Coronavirus times), and people are resorting to online shopping. Countless Disney stores have been closed due to the novel concentration of shifting to online shopping, at ShopDisney.com. I remember when Zara closed down stores, and I myself resorted to apps of both of these.

Encoding/ Decoding – Stuart Hall – A message, traditionally in communication, has a sender and a receiver. This is axiomatic and self-explanatory at best, but venturing further into it, I am acknowledging there can be myriad and subtle issues that go completely unnoticed and unrecognized. The message can be woefully misinterpreted or distorted through no one's fault. A message in fashion is characteristically and expectedly understated or subtle, but this can be so problematic. It is codified and encoded by the sender and decoded by the receiver (Hall, 2001.) This process can be nullified when the message is distorted. There has to be a valid and comprehensible meaning. Without meaning, Hall suggests, there cannot be 'consumption' (164.)

In different occasions, you dress accordingly. You emulate different things, even icons of music or popular culture. In different settings, you 'wear different hats', that is: you act accordingly in so many ways that become the norm of that moment. In fashion, you dressing speaks unfathomable, unimaginable volumes about you and for you. You inadvertently might be saying things that are more susceptible to being distorted. You are misconstrued if you are not careful, so be smart about dressing. Be bespoke about style. The way one decodes you, even through your dress, doesn't represent the authentic "you", but it does talk about how **you are presenting that "you" at the time.**

Articulation – Antonio Gramsci – One of the best uses of this theory is how fashion (when we use a critical lens) can be described as an appropriator of culture or guilty of "cultural appropriation", which is essentially taking parts of a culture and assimilating them to your culture in an inappropriate way. That is my definition of cultural appropriation. It involves **hegemony**, or cultural dominance by perhaps the elite or most hierarchically influential group, because the hegemonic group uses the other culture without being part of it. It does not comprehend the practices of the culture, and it takes from it, according to Cambridge Online Dictionary (n.d.) It may happen by someone naïve or unbeknownst, but it is certainly disrespectful and distasteful. Examples of cultural appropriation are Urban Outfitters branding its products as Navajo or committed in popular culture by celebrities like Justin Bieber or Kim Kardashian sporting cornrows. It (in my humble opinion) is so normalized and ingrained in our society that it is an overlooked problem. People are increasingly desensitized and essentially numb to it.

Anyway, Gramsci's ideas are rooted in his sociological concept of **superstructure**, but more resonant and consistent with this train of thought of cultural appropriation might very well be the concept of hegemony. It follows, then, that Gramsci postulated the ruling class determines what political and ideological pathways a society will embark on. He supposes that internally, society is disintegrated through "controls of every kind" (Gramsci, 2010, pg. 265)

SYMBOLIC INTERACTIONISM – sociological – This is the impact of language and linguistics on social being. Symbolic interactionism emphasizes the livelihood of meaning, a socially constructed and subjective.

FUNCTIONALISM – aesthetic or social-psychological – In social psychology, it is a generic and umbrella term for a school of thought; it is the idea that all aspects of a society can be utilized to prove their usefulness. In fashion or art, it is the idea that an item should be designed upon its use and functionality rather than aesthetic or artistic considerations. In both realms, it intertwines and expresses the same doctrine or dogma: use.

Cultural Identity theory – It was coined by Mary Jane Collier and Milt Thomas in 1988. It proposes the very immanent idea that a person is accepted into a group that resonates with the same meanings, symbols, emblems, etc. (Chen & Lin, 2016.)

Expectancy Violations theory – In its most primitive and basic terms, this theory resounds with a belief I am invested in inextricably:

image, although it not everything, is the first thing people see. It was originally used to approach nonverbal communication, which in fashion is eminent. People make judgements off of your appearance and mine, every day. This is unavoidable and inescapable. People make judgments (however presumptuous) based on looks and descriptors that come to mind instantaneously when meeting someone. People have expectations that can be affirmed or violated. There are generally consequences in both scenarios. These expectations can be culturally dictated and pertain to time and haptics (space.) They also rely on social norms. The more deviant a violation seems, the higher the extent of the consequence or the consequences that occur (Burgoon, 2015.) In the fashion milieu, I believe this theory can be prominent and useful if employed. We are vigilant and act like guards to our appearance, but we comment (however vocally or even inadvertently) on the appearance or fashion choices or accessories (or the process of this) of others.

Identity Management theory – social science/ communication – coined by Tadasu Todd-Imahori and William R. Cupach in 2005. Essentially, Imahori and Cupach (2005) postulate that one needs to have a negotiation with their identity in order to finetune it in the intercultural communication process. Everyone needs to understand this identity in a mutual, collective process. Managing relational and cultural identities, people reflect their own identity by their management of communication. "IMT concerns the process of affording people who are involved in interpersonal communication in intercultural contexts a confirmation of self-esteem and self-efficacy in their identity" (Chen & Lin, 2016, pg. 5.) In fashion, this is vital. Why? It is so, because image is what people see first and what people instinctively judge as person by. It is an endlessly reflexive process, thus, and it involves reciprocity. Self-esteem manifests itself in fashion, sublimating itself as well. Self-esteem and self-efficacy show through image and how one carries him- or herself; this is part of fashion.

Co-cultural theory – Co-cultural theory was postulated by Mark Orbe (Chen & Lin, 2006.) This is more political (not in a conventional definition of politics) in the way that it is critical of hierarchical dominance of one group over another. In fashion, we see an ingroup (kids or people practicing the trend, the fad, generally what is popular) and the outgroup (anarchists or people just going against the system or trend; these people get ostracized.)

Social identity theory – This theory approaches a person with the presumed understanding that they belong to a social organization (Chen & Lin, 2016.) This brings to my mind the outgroup (alienated people) and the ingroup (the assimilated, usually gratified, people.) Being critical of subcultures and preconceived notions about rebels and anarchists come to mind. This is a tremendous terrain in fashion where this theory could be made use of. The resistance to being defined by a group one belongs to (such as goth or punk) is what this theory resembles to me. Even though this theory considers social categories, it considers them of the group. The member's beliefs are considered, but I believe the member is read as an assimilated part of the group. The member's beliefs and values are most likely defined or related to the group's values.

Cultural evolutionary theory – Social change occurs as we go on. Social changes is accelerated or catalyzed by socialization and social transmission. It is informed by changes and unavoidably changes in the world, climate change for example, and the advent of technology and social media; fashion evolves or is hindered by such occurrences and issues as well.

IDENTITY NEGOTIATION THEORY (INT) – interpersonal communication – Identity negotiation theory is explained as identity being a mix of identities. "The term identity in the Identity Negotiation Theory (INT) refers to an individual's multifaceted identities of cultural, ethnic, religious, social class, gender, sexual orientation, professional, family/relational role, and personal image(s) based on self-reflection and other-categorization social construction processes" (Ting-Toomy, 2015, pg. 1.)

Stuart Hall's identity - Identities incessantly change and happen to waver. They are not a matter of static being but transitional, transient "becoming", and ideology (Hall, 1996.)

DISTINCTION – social science – Pierre Bourdieu – I have taken distinction to inherently suggest and go hand-in-hand with social stratification. Through tastes, as this theory says, people ascertain their superiority or inferiority. They create a hierarchical structure. Not knowing the total extent of such a theory, I do not know if it suggests tyranny as a consequence. A person at hand defines and establishes their likes, dislikes, interests, and tastes through distinction.

ROLE THEORY – Role theory can help us to relate dress as part of the roles we regularly play Miller-Spellman & Riley 2019.) Our roles are in relation to social relationships and other people or groups. It is guided by our attitudes and knowledge and I would add dispositions and temperaments.

COLLECTIVE SELECTION THEORY – this is a theory that is intimately related to the field of fashion. Our choices in life dictate our fashion choices. These are initially developed by word-of-mouth interactions and media to name a few factors (Miller-Spellman & Riley, 2019.)

DRAMATURGICAL APPROACH – We have possibly all heard the Shakespeare quote that all the world's a stage. I definitely view us as mere actors on this world stage. It is where we can involve theater in social contexts and ultimately in fashion. How we play actors in the stage of the world or its many stages and platforms can be studied through the dramaturgical approach. It situates us as players in life being played out on a stage (Miller-Spellman & Riley, 2019.) Goffman came up with this theory, a sociological one, and I think I would liken the audiences that we dictate our actions by to masses that we cater to in fashion.

I am trying to coin some theories or terms here; let's see how it goes!

Selection heuristic – The selection heuristic relates directly to the collective selection theory and paradox of choice. The paradox of choice is that there are usually multiple things to choose from; there is actually so much to choose from that more effort goes into choosing (Schwartz, 2004.) It can cause anxiety and can overwhelm us. It depends chiefly on six factors, as I outline.

CAPITAL – all kinds of capital are involved, but primarily cultural and symbolic capital are involved. Your choices are influenced by your values, attitudes, and behaviors. Behavioristic data, incidentally, is included with these to navigate consumerism and consumer behavior (Clodfelter, 2018.) Symbolically, capital of an intangible form is involved. When we use symbols in whatever medium we are communicating, we use a lexicon. The symbols are ingrained in us and consequently influence our choices.

IMPULSIVITY – We all know there term "impulse buy." I also was introduced to the term, "buying mood" some time ago. These intertwine to create impulsivity. As a perpetual or habitual part of us, impulsivity influences our choices by how much we are thinking. Usually, we can attribute the impulse buy to the moment and its intensity. We just had to have that item, so we were not thinking.

EXPENDABILITY – Now, the next factor is spending, so do not get them confused. Expendability is how disposable your **financial resources** are. This is how much you have to spend on fashions.

SPENDING – Spending is broader than expendability. It also involves how much effort, time, and mental resources we utilize when shopping. We can put something in our cart, in person or online, and we can change our mind later. This is when we see that time has been spent, and effort as well has been used. We can tire of shopping, and it is because we spend that effort, time, and mental capacity on browsing racks or websites.

POWER – This is not spending power, as a disclaimer; this is privilege and position. Power is just how it manifests itself. We can sit at the top of a hierarchy or "food chain" or at the bottom, even in the middle somewhere, but it influences our choices. The socioeconomic status and rank we hold also feeds power, and this power shapes our perspective and horizons. This influences our tastes and who we do or do not emulate in fashion.

GEOPOLITICS – Of course, we have to consider location, but in a wider context, it is the setting where the choice and shopping occur. Politics of the place *in situ*, or in a natural or original habitat, influence us. We, in turn, make choices in shopping based on geopolitics. It can be local or global or international, and how all of this interacts impacts how we shop.

The next theory I propose is very obvious. It might not even be that original on my account, but it needs a name. It is the consumer-designer theory.

CONSUMER-DESGINER THEORY – The fashion world is seeing consumers and designers coming together. The consumers dictate trends, and designers listen to the consumers, thusly creating a collaboration between the two. Consumers should be perceptive, imaginative, and insightful, so the designers can cater with clarity and sanity.

SOCIAL ACTOR THEORY –On the social media platform, all of its platforms, there is outreach and influencer marketing. This is a way people act socially in their videos, having a conversation with global citizens of the fashion world. What that means is all of the fashion-conscious people that reside in this borderless world.

VACUUM-VISION THEORY – Our vision is clouded by disarming and misleading ideals. We need to be wary and vigilant of this. We cannot forget the context in which fashion is being circulated; we also need to consider in what form it is being circulated; for example as a trend and what type of trend. We have to envision the world without being clouded by too many "clues"; we want to read clues cautiously, within their setting and with keeping in mind that fashion does not exist in a vacuum (sorry to use that cliché.)

What are the best research methods to use in fashion?

There is object-based research, semiotics or semiology, interviews, ethnography and online ethnography, and survey research. Secondarily, there are ethnomethodology (not to be conflated with or confused with ethnography), oral history, audio-visual studies and documentations, cross-cultural studies (that help apply global and transnational themes), and triangulation (moreover used to legitimize and solidify our empirical research. I want to add interviewing and polls. I want to investigate what kind of questions are best to ask in fashion.

OBJECT BASED RESEARCH

According to Kawamura (2020), object-based research is more likely to be used be art historians, curators, and costume historians than sociologists or economists. Since it is material, tangible research following what I would say is very concrete pathways, object-based research is utilized by those that dealt with fashion, art, culture in a tactile manner. Also, clothing from yesteryear is primary. Ancillary evidence is not necessarily less reliable or less telling, but I would say that primary sources are historical and possibly more authentic in respect to the time period being studied.

Object-based research makes comparisons more refined and more convenient. With an interconnecting type of approach, this type of research begs other insightful questions that can manifest physically or mentally, and it seeks to understand relationships. According to Kawamura (2020), object-based research examines "minute details" and is "interpretive" (p. 93.) She highlights how conservation becomes important here. Display and presentation become vital factors as well. Maintaining a presentable look for an artifact is corollary to curation; it becomes rudimental.

A limitation Kawamura cites for object-based research is myopia to aesthetic details and focus limited to "physical considerations" (2020, pg. 93.) With an approach to material and culture, it seeks to elucidate meanings behind emblems and symbols in fashion and art. It can be combined with other methods, like oral histories, to weave narratives (Kawamura, 2020.)

What is semiotics? What is semiology?

The fashion world is always flowing and cohering. Ideas and terms are defined and redefined when they encounter each other. The nuanced idea that nothing is fixed in fashion points to the idea that words are multilayered to describe different things. Conversely, myriad words can describe one thing, and it differs by brands. Whatever the language is (of the brand, branding, promotion, etc.) or what have you, it is decipherable by semiology and symbolisms. The underlying meanings can be unpacked amply and tellingly.

I was introduced to this ideal in my undergraduate study, with Saussure and Geertz being the mainstay figures in the realm. He viewed language and its composition as a system. Etymology and genealogy of words and families struck him. The rules of language and the rights and wrongs can be societally imposed, according to Ferdinand de Saussure.

Geertz took a notably more cultural approach than a societal one. He said language is loaded with meaning of culture.

Roland Barthes is a figure whose books I own, "The Fashion System" and "The Language of Fashion." Yuniya Kawamura (2020) cites his contributions and work. Barthes contributed by conducting a study of language in fashion; it is documented in his book "The Fashion System" (1990.) Barthes implies that the clothes' analyses and descriptions are what ultimately indicate or decide whether the garment is fashion or not, in the eyes of the public. In Saussure's words, words are signified and arbitrary. The need to be given meaning. An example is a tree. When one thinks of a tree, they will think of leaves or branches. Color that generically come to mind are green and brown. Is this, then, what signifies the "tree-ness" of the tree? In fashion, we could say myriad things. We can talk about the composition, shape, color, name, descriptors, perception, etc. of the garment. That can all be endemic of it. "Boat-neck", "scoop neck", "v-neck", and "crewneck" are descriptors that can be given to a top. Then we can describe its hem as raw, asymmetrical, etc. These are the aesthetic or material descriptors of it, and affects it elicits are more subjective and theoretical.

INTERVIEWING

Interviews can take several forms; of these are "semi-structured" and "unstructured" interviews (Brennen, 2013.) Questions can be difficult and tedious, but assuredly, they reflect your abilities and reciprocate by getting you quality answers when done right. They can get personal and that can create awkwardness. One strategy Brennon (2013) mentions is to depersonalize the questions by making them third-person. Try to always encourage authentic, utilizable answers (Brennen, 2013.) You need to get answers that are insightful and valuable. Craft the questions, and the rest is ancillary. This isn't as complicated later on as it is at first. It sounds simple, really; just questions... but in the long-run, crafting them is not just tedious, it is challenge at times. Get respondents that can provide such answers and please pay attention to the nonverbal cues that you are exhibiting during your interview (Brennen, 2013.)

You want to implement icebreakers in the beginning, and these will include the research you have done (Brennen, 2013.) You can ask probing questions. You can ask a personal question, and you can strategize these too seem more omniscient and less intimate. You also want to ask filtering questions; you don't want your mental space cluttered or discombobulated, and you don't want to be overwhelmed or confused. An example is filtering your materials when tracking a trend: you want to ask what the newest ideas are and if it makes sense to a lay person. If not, you should provide more compelling examples of it. Your sources of information and inspiration cam be art or music but should be substantial and strong. You also need to think ahead and predict how or if it can give rise to new products (Holland & Jones, 2017.)

Here is an example of some interview questions I created; I did not administer them. It is always important to administer them to the right person, so consider this deeply!

Interview Questions:

1. In your opinion, does fashion stratify society's member from each other? It is more mental or physical or both. How does this happen?
2. Do trends alienate the people that do not follow them? How so?
3. Does fashion, moreover, create boundaries or bridge gaps?
4. How does fashion transcend borders or boundaries?
5. Which hierarchies does fashion create?
6. What are the potential risks associated with not being part of a trend or a movement in the fashion world?
7. What power relations and perceptions of power are created by apparel and/ or accessories used?
8. How reflective of your tastes is how you dress daily? How much consideration goes into it?

Here are two examples of interviews I did:

The first one deals with an issue that has risen to prominence recently. It is close to my heart, as it should be! Anyway, I interviewed Black business owner and designer of Rekless Creations, Brittany Wongus, about a tee she designed that fights alongside the movement. I applaud her greatly for her work in this realm.

The second one is a more general interview I did spotlighting her brand. In the interview, I asked her about her process, trends, and her mindset. Then I asked her about the Video Girl tee she designed.

US: Describe your involvement with the Black Lives Matter Movement.

BW: My role in the 'Black Lives Matter Movement" is to spread the message through art. Not only are the customers purchasing a Revolution tee, they are donating as well. For every tee purchased, half of the proceeds go towards Protest Bail Out.

US: Why is fashion, namely Rekless Creations, a powerful way to fight alongside this movement?

BW: People want a statement piece, wearable art that reflects their feelings, their vibe, and who they are as an individual. Rekless Creations is that brand that has no censor at all.

US: How has the existence of the brand helped you process the latest occurrences in police brutality?

BW: I have processed the police brutality through social media, listening to artists who talk about police brutality such as NWA, public enemy, and watching documentaries.

Police brutality is very frequently in the urban community.

US: Explain the intent behind the Black Lives Matter tee and its slogans.

BW: The intent behind the BLM tee was to tell everyone, black, Hispanic, Caucasian, natives, whoever! that it is time for a revolution. Racism, police brutality are ongoing issues in the world, not just in the United States. We have to come together as one because we are all humans; no one should be degraded because of the pigment of their skin. Change is coming and we as the people have the power to make that change.

US: How does the tee call for solidarity?

BW: The Revolution Tee calls for solidarity because everyone is ready for evolution.

US: In what ways would you say the tee is political, and in what ways is it not?

BW: The tee is political because we are in a human rights war.

This movement has a lot to do with politics from police enforcement, racism, economic issues like poverty, unemployment, etc.

US: What are the other avenues in art and fashion that can help fight systemic racism?

BW: These certain avenues would be, but are not limited to, donations, powerful sayings on apparel, and giving equal opportunities.

US: What feelings has this process brought you? How did you cope with it with fashion?

BW: The day that George Floyd was murdered, my heart was heavy with anger, frustration, and sadness which led me to pour all that emotion into the Revolution Tee. I did a spin-off of the Time magazine; basically "Time" is a political magazine that I needed to bring in the focus of that. I used the fist to represent the people coming together. Under the fist you have different sayings like, 'Being black is not a crime',' change is coming' and 'power to the people' which leads us to a Revolution.

Fashion has always been there to reassure us, and not only can it help give us a voice and platform for issues, but it helps us have healing at times when we need it. Fashion can vocalize the ineffable and materialize the intangible. It captures the elusive things we confront and gives words in other forms that we never knew we needed. It blocks the normalization of racism in this case, and it does wonders for us. Fashion should typically serve as a vocal platform for issues and movements, especially Black Lives Matter, and it should also prove to be an expressive and liberating one as well.

Brittany has made some salient and very insightful points in this interview. Minds like her make us feel like this world is headed in a much-needed direction. She believes in social media, watching documentaries and calling for change in the form of donations, apparel, and equal opportunities, as you can see. Rekless Creations can be shopped at www.reklesscreations.com and the Instagram handle for the brand is simply @reklesscreations. You can also follow the brand on Facebook, where it is also titled "Rekless Creations."

Second interview:

Brittany Wongus, founder and designer at "Rekless Creations", has a truly wondrous mind that envisions a world that encompasses urban wear and art as a whole. Championing fashion in the city and urban contexts, she transcends barriers, catering to a wide audience while providing an enticing and authentic voice for social, cultural, and artistic life.

Fashion has become more than just aesthetics. It has always been a multidimensional interactive and creative process, providing platforms and outlets for social expression. Now, more than ever, it is needed to be seen for that value. A universal, timeless, and transcendent approach, clothing and purchasing behavior reflect attitudes of consumers that underground fashion namely, urban wear, deals with. An authentic means for a voice and art through one's styling and fashion is urban wear. A profile on the Philadelphia-based urban wear brand, "Rekless Creations", this article veers deeply into the imaginative mind of founder, owner, designer, and innovator Brittany Wongus.

US: Where did you grow up, and what were the most influential memories from it?

BW: I was born and raised in Philadelphia, PA. My mom was always taking part in the creative arts and culture, so I was inspired by that. Philadelphia itself has a culture of go-getter people and creative people. I was also into music and history, since Philadelphia is a city of history and is a known city for that. Growing up in Philadelphia inspired me to go after my passion.

US: Where do you typically draw inspiration from?

BW: I draw inspiration from music. I have two go-to genres, which are neo-soul and hip hop. They help me visualize and create. I take from the words, or rather lyrics. I also take from the instruments and sounds of the instruments.

US: What typically goes through your mind during the creative process?

BW: Well, I certainly have a vision to start. I want to create an abstract art piece. What amazes me about art and fashion is that everyone can have their own interpretation or perspective of it. There is not one definition of the pieces, and I am also not going for just one definition of the piece; I want there to be more. There is diversity in perception.

US: Why is it increasingly important to keep cultural and artistic values on the forefront—especially in a dramatically and increasingly polarized world?

BW: It is definitely important. There are means of expression and to speak up. We live in a world where we are slowly being stripped of our freedoms, and we find our freedoms from being artistic.

US: What unique messages can urban fashion embody and communicate—with a platform and milieu of its own?

BW: I feel like it is mostly about attitude and expression and just not regarding anything. You do what you want and dress how you want.

US: To what extent is the outlet of fashion imaginative or elaborate? What limitations can urban fashion challenge or break?

BW: Well, my response to this question would have to be modeled after a saying. They say you can't wear white after Labor Day. I like to defy this, for example. I think it's all about giving a spotlight to how you feel and just have no rules. You even need to break the rules.

US: What is "Rekless Creations" primarily? What does it stand for?

BW: "Rekless Creations" is about having no limitations to you, to your art, and to your creativity.

US: How is "Rekless Creations" marketable to masses of people? Who does it cater to?

BW: I wouldn't say who it caters to. I would just say it sends out a great message; the elements really blend in with the meaning behind the brand. People should follow their own trends and promote the underground, artistic scene in this way.

US: How do you navigate emerging trends in the culture of consumers, consumerism, and in consumer behavior? What are the looking for and how do you engage with such needs?

BW: The consumers that engage with "Rekless Creations" want something new and do not follow any trend. They want something different to add to their wardrobe and start a new trend. Let me put it like this: I really would say consumer and customers are their own artists and the choices they make reflect that.

US: How does "Rekless Creations" adapt to an everchanging, ageless fashion world of ideas, concepts, and buying trends and habits?

BW: Well, I just keep in mind constantly that trends are changing and so are ideas. Of course, like I have been saying, people should go ahead and create their own trend. I keep in touch with the most current issues. As the brand expands, these ideals are to be kept in mind. History, even fashion, repeats itself, so that is another important idea I keep in mind.

US: What are your initial and long-term thoughts on the future of "Rekless Creations"?

BW: It is becoming a household and international name, and it is being revolutionary at the same time. It is making a change in fashion and the fashion world.

US: What piece of "Rekless Creations" clothing has been the most enjoyable and rewarding for you to create? Please elaborate on why you would choose this item.

BW: I would definitely have to say that is the Video Girl tee. It was inspired by Andy Warhol. It deals with a really sensitive subject, so I am proud I put it out. Women are incredibly sexualized, and it was great to make an abstract statement about that going on. It sold out very quickly, but I love it so much that soon I am going to bring it back out.

US: Lastly, what has been most inspiring to you—the creative processes or then the results that you have seen from "Rekless Creations"? Why?

BW: I would say both the creative process and the result equally inspire me to go further. I research a lot, like colors and garments. I put the color onto the garments and mix and match, which is how I visualize the end result. This is my creative process. I then want to see how people react and respond to the result of this, and of course, I want to see how this reflects on their purchasing behaviors. When you make something that is to cater to the public and they like it, that is an exciting feeling. It is just great to be rewarded when you put in so much effort.

Rekless Creations has been instrumental, presently, in the fashion game, contesting boundaries and defying trends. The latest ventures have been pop-up shops and the unveiling of the "Express Yourself" tee. Rekless Creations can be shopped at www.reklesscreations.com, and the blog is available at www.rcembrace.com.

Thanks goes to Brittany Wongus for sitting for the interview.

ETHNOGRAPHY

Ethnography originates from studies of culture and anthropology. It chiefly deals with interaction between people of different cultures (Brennen, 2013.) "Ethnography focuses on believe and think, and how they live their daily lives. It is used to answer questions about people's beliefs, rituals, attitudes, actions, stories, and behaviors, emphasizing what people actually do rather than what they say they do" (Brennen, 2013, pg. 166.) It is an immersive technique, meaning the researcher(s) intermix(es) with a group by living among that group, whether it be a religion or a cultural group or social group or a society. It inquires about ways of living and thriving and echoes the cliché that actions speak louder than words. It focuses on the rituals (or habits or actions) of the group at hand.

I would add that ethnography builds strong ties and relationships to diversified groups. It leads, collectively, to a larger and more elucidated understanding of a group and the observer. In fashion, ethnography can be manifest in the form of sitting with students that dress a certain way, subcultures to be more precise. It builds narratives that can be applied universally, but of course, it cannot be applied incorrectly on the whole.

Online research and online ethnography are tools I have used in my research. For example: I studied comments Pakistanis made about women and the #MeToo movement, when an actress was courageous to come forward and give her story to the public. I studied social media and other online blogs, forums, and platforms. In fashion, this is a useful tool that can study hashtags that fashion deals with. It can study movements that fashion deals with, like #NoH8, #BlackLivesMatter, #MeToo, etc.

SURVEY RESEARCH

What comes to your mind when you think of a survey? I think of questions. What is a synonym for survey? I do not know if I can clearly delineate for it a synonym, but a very related word would be questionnaire. Surveys are abundant due to their usefulness in research. They can yield data and appeal to the emotions as well as engage insightfully by asking for this emotion and feeling. They can produce quantitative and qualitative results.

EXAMPLE OF A Survey (not administered):
Appendix C:

Survey Questions:

Surveys are administered to women and men of differing ages and origins. This is not to simulate difference or comparison, but it is to gain a broader perspective overall of people that engage with fashion. People engage on different levels, but fashion is a sphere that everyone takes part in.

Section 1: Demographic information:

1. Age
2. Ethnicity
3. Sex
4. Gender identity

Section 2: Upbringing

5. I was raised in an
   a. Low-Income Household
   b. Middle-Class Household
6. I would say I attribute my upbringing to
   a. Urban settings
   b. Affluent settings
7. Growing up, most of my time was spent
   a. Outdoors
   b. Indoors
8. I occupied most of my time with: **CHECK ALL THAT APPLY**
   a. Sports
   b. Reading/ Writing
   c. Other
9. I was always most inclined towards: **CHECK ONE ONLY**
   a. Athletic pursuits (playing sports, working out, etc.)
   b. Intellectual pursuits (school and grades, reading and writing, learning, enlightening myself, etc.)

c. Social pursuits (being spiritual and/ or religious, having friends, being occupied with social media, being involved in family, etc.)
d. Cultural pursuits (Music events, culinary, museums, being fashionable, film and TV, etc.)
e. Other
10. In school and college/ University life, I was in the following types of student organizations:
a. Fashion and art (Couture club, art clubs, etc.)
b. Cultural (Best Buddies, gay/ straight alliance, etc.)
c. Religious/ Spiritual (Areligious club, Atheist/ Agnostic clubs, Muslim Students Association, Christian or Catholic Students Association, Hindu Students Club, etc.)
d. Ethnic/ racial clubs (Pakistani Students Association, Latin Students Association, Hispanic Students Association, Asian Students Union, American-Indian Students Association, Black Students Association, etc.)

Section 3: Tastes

11. I usually like food that is:
a. Spicy or savory
b. Sweet
c. Sour
12. The music I listen to can best be described as: **CHECK ONE ONLY**
a. Indie/ Alternative/ Rock
b. Pop
c. Hip Hop/ Rap
d. EDM
e. Other
13. In movies, I usually watch: **CHECK ONE ONLY**
a. Animated (Disney, etc.)
b. Comedy

FASHION: ASPECTS, PROCESSES, THOUGHTS, METHODS

   c. Romantic Comedies
   d. Romance
   e. Drama
   f. Thriller/ Suspense
   g. Horror
   h. Other
14. My favorite TV show is:

15. My favorite place to shop (for clothes) is:

   a. High-end retailers
   b. Affordable retailers
   c. Designer labels
   d. Thrift-shopping
   e. Online only platforms
   f. Other

16. Consider your favorite clothing store, what is it?

17. Consider your favorite clothing brand, what is it?

III

VIGNETTES 1. Identity 2. Time 3. Inspiration: INS

How important is it to stand out in the fashion milieu/ fashion world?

It cannot be stressed, at least in my view, enough. I feel like blending in is too banal or too bland. You want to be noticed and praised. You want to be distinguishable, distinct, and characteristic. You want to brand yourself and trademark yourself. If you do not do this, there are possibly dire consequences. You risk anonymity. I may not be coining a **new** term with this, but I am reiterating an indispensable, vital, and even probably rudimental concept with this conversation—mind you (readers and thinkers) a concept very engrained in our daily interactions. Anonymity can create paranoia and ambiguity, to start. Simply, it is too commonplace and makes a person unnecessarily common. Being unnecessarily common means that a person does not even have an identity, and they can stand out however and whenever desired. They certainly do not need to be or to stay anonymous. They can easily ascertain and mold an identity and even (if need) reinvent it, but that is a different conversation that may appear later on.

Anonymity is one of those things where I can assuredly attribute it to a cliché or two. *It is that crucial and risky. Be careful what you wish for. You've bitten off more than you can chew.*

Does fashion enable us to be anonymous/ blend in, or does it moreover encourage individuality?

This is a difficult question that would require deep intuition and thorough investigation, not to mention an unfathomable philosophical and critical approach. I am a philosophical person most of the time, but to this question, I am doubting my answer would even suffice.

Anyway, while I have posed the question, it is really entertaining, revealing, and enriching to answer questions we pose ourselves; in this realm, it is exponentially and growingly important to be inquisitive and unrelentingly so.

Enough jargon and jibber-jabber, let us delve into the question. I think, personally, the simple answer (not objective because that is impossible here) is the fashion gives us, endows us, with individuality AND affiliation. That is the beauty of it. It can be wondrously and insightfully dichotomous! We can blend in, and when we choose not to, we strategically do not. It is advantageous to say the least! Fashion immanently makes us stand out too. We can blend in AND SIMULTANEOUSLY stand out. We can be trendsetters of groups we belong to, and that is the most succinct example of this.

What could necessitate (incidentally, anecdotally rather than objectively) the need to reinvent yourself in fashion? Is it necessary—how necessary?

Negotiating and contextualizing oneself in an evergreen, evolutionary, everchanging world is necessitated and also necessitates fashion. It **is not always** necessary. It is not a corollary or a livelihood. When one can reinvent their self, it is an awesome way to experiment, but I would say I have never favored it and always seen it as direly dangerous and unassumingly, subtly, but assuredly and powerfully uncertain and as a territory that we cannot easily tread on and makes us increasingly uneasy. Why all of these crazily strong words for this?

Reinventing ourselves is intrinsically uncertain. It causes us to be unaware—of who we are—and unbeknownst—to who we can be. It makes us obsequious—to people using us (I'll explain this), and it makes us susceptible—to being subordinated and/ or submissive. People can find us as easy targets or impressionable targets when we try to "reinvent" ourselves. How? Well, if you consider it, can't this willingness to let the way you define yourself be in limbo do that? In retrospect I have ascertained my extroverted, stylish, Disney-loving, fashion-and-art-appreciating self as eccentric and incomprehensible. No one can define me or use me, but if you let others define you (because reinventing yourself will certainly involve this) you will be an easier target to be "used." I don't recommend it one bit, but to others, it poses a picture of favorability and freedom. It inspired (not authenticity) but creativity. I would conclude my position cantankerously and firmly, but I would attribute this to being like a "double-edge sword." It has its ups and downs; it has its advantages and disadvantages.

Time

They say time is money. It is precious and invaluable, as it makes everything able to be marked and makes things measurable. It is expressed in numbers, so it is quantifiable; it is a way to track and trace virtually everything you can come across. This should be what is meant when "they" (people) say time is money: that it is profusely elucidating, and that makes aspects of life infinitely and indispensably more communicable and convenient. It is objective and fixed when it is numerical and concrete. In abstract expressions like esoteric, endemic temporality or transience, it takes on subjectivity and intertextuality (where it is read in myriad ways and given myriad contexts and meanings.) As it becomes interpreted and symbolic, it also becomes perpetuated. With this all considered, then, shall we consider fashion's time more objective or subjective? The answer is resounding yes and affirming no! Why? Because it deals with both. Considering there are 52 seasons on the calendar of fashion and considering the past as it has to be taken, it can be objective. The negating of this is by subjective means. What I mean to say is that they clash but also coexist; it is paradoxical. Objective time allows for subjective time to exist. Subjective time is fluid and deems everything wavering and meaningful. It can cause the past to be reinterpreted, recontextualized, and examined. It can cause for history to be the driving force for the future, after all, to restate a cliché, history does repeat itself! In social science, just to add parenthetically (but not peripherally), chronemics is the word for time. Time has rules and is arguably not fixed. Culturally there are rules (Adler, Proctor II, & Rosenfeld, 2010.) These can easily intertwine to explain phenomena in fashion. Just like I said for space, time wavers. Occasions waver. Rules are ascertained and reaffirmed through expectations, and we know there are engrained expectations in fashion, here in the United States, and globally. Violating these expectations brings in one of the theories I have discussed (expectancy violations theory or EVT.) The same can be said for haptics, or space.

    Clothes can be symptomatic of time, prescient or indicative of the future or present time, and imprinted statements and/ or imprints. They can tell stories of the past, present, and future and of all things that speak to us and about us or about things dear to us that we cherish or covet. They insightfully, retrospectively, and revealingly tell of time and setting and society. They can be bold and vibrant, even radiating minimalism (as this is a statement in itself: that "less is more.") They are constantly imprinted with and burdened with the responsibility of speaking about time and location and of ownership, commodification, and communication; these will all (at some point) resonate heavily with time.

What embodies time in fashion? Does it get disembodied? What embodies it other than the 52 seasons in a fashion calendar, the zeitgeist and decades that defined fashion, the recurring trends and effort to revive a trend (funny I say that, because you pretty much cannot revive a dead trend), or short-term fads or classics that take on an endlessly long lifespan? Can we think of other aspects of artistic expression, like fashion, that are embodied—err—even disembodied? Art is also defined by periods and decades, and as it intertwines with fashion in ineffably many ways, it gives way to fashion's periods and decades. These seem to repeat. The neon colors, scrunchies, stirrup pants, flappers, long-hair, grunge, punk, flannels, gothic subculture, and zootsuits and more: these define periods and subcultures in fashion; some of them repeat. These are more recent than Nehru jackets and Victorian dresses, which made marks in different parts of the world. In my experience as a Pakistani American, I see that designers like Deepak Perwani and the "Lollywood" film industry of Pakistan still deal with Nehru jackets and banhgalas (similar to those) and Indian designers and Bollywood do too.

Intergenerational Factors and Gaps

Fashion seeps into all routines. It not only helps us navigate but explicate this unfathomable, labyrinthine life and narrativize and simplify it. The different ideas and doubts its poses are embodied in the generational and intergenerational complications and nuances we are socialized into. They become symbolic and endemic to us.

Millennials have different issues and amass different resources and fashions to approach these issues. So do baby boomers, Generation X, and Gen Z (Zoomers). Milennials garner ample attention nowadays, as they are the generation having to deal with crises and (arguably to me) feelings of emptiness and feeling devoid and detached. They will (just like everyone else) have to deal unavoidably with the fallout of the COVID-19 era we currently occupy and inhabit. I am a millennial, and I know there will be feelings of dejection and ups and downs. Admittedly I am quite uncertain about the future at times, but I use retail therapy and fashion theory to get me through it. It gives me hope for the future, embodying evolution and change. It can be revolutionary, and this is a rejoicing factor. It innately provides tools and platforms to protest inequities and disruptions to society in gender and race. It can be clothing or no clothing, and it certainly drives positivity.

Walking Billboards, Walking Resumes: An Aside

We are deemed useless (by arguably others and ourselves) when we are not productive. Personally, when I am not being prolific or productive, I feel dejected, inert, and stagnant. This section is not as concerned with clothes as it is with expectations. These can be harmfully and incredibly intrusive and voyeuristic, presumptuous and overwhelming, etc. These cause, as Anne Helen Peterson (2020) argues in her book, *Can't Even: How Millennials became the Burnout Generation*, burnout.

She says we turn out to have these expectations that transform us into walking resumes. How does fashion factor in? Well, just as they say "we are judged by the company we keep", we are also judged from our clothes. Susan Sontag (1964) says in "Against Interpretation", that interpretation is "reactionary" and "stifling" (p. 5.) We are walking billboards and walking resumes. These work together, as we advertise ourselves and our (not really qualifications) details, both cultivated and inborn, by our characteristic look, mannerisms, and style. If we dress lazily, we will be interpreted as such; please do not ever confuse this with "effortless" style or dressing "effortlessly." I draw an extremely fine line and make these two utterly distinguishable. Effortless style can be innate, but lazy style must be lackadaisical. A person who dresses conservatively and uses understated expression is being business-like, both with mannerism and attire; they will expectedly be interpreted as such. Leisurely style can attribute itself to athleisure and signify going to the gym or having gone to the gym.

Material Things: *Another Aside*

Maybe we go through life collecting material things so we can prolong a congenital and characteristic connection to fashion, what it has given us, and what is has innocuously deprived us of. Perhaps it is fainty, indistinctly, indiscriminately reminiscent of those (of what it has taken away.)

First, this connection is personal, rather than impersonal. It is somewhat arbitrary and imperfect. It is human. It is vocal in that way. Fashion speaks volumes to us and about us without moving a muscle. The connection one has in invisible most of the time. It is perhaps most visible when one looks into their closet or another's wardrobe and characterizes their own or their peer's style. It also become visible when shopping.

There are some unnamable things fashion tirelessly and endlessly endows us with. These certain things are innumerable, so I cannot provide a whole list, but I will provide a wholesome one. Fashion gives us:

- Purpose: it is systemic and individual at the same time. It can be individualistic and highly personal and attributable to someone and institutionalized and collectivistic at the same time. In fact, that what it is. It gives meaning, not only in communication, but in ourselves. It makes our own situations, schemas, and responses more understandable. It gives us sociological purpose and social-psychological purpose. What I mean to allude to is how it exists in so many spaces in so many dimensions, giving us meaning and individuality while also representing our affiliation with groups (religious, cultural, ethnic, ideological, etc.) and factions.
- Belonging: it situates us in this vast, intricate world as members of the entire world and network and community of the world. Through engaging in fashion, we belong to countless groups and inculcate ourselves into groups and outgroups. We go with and against the trend to strengthen bonds to humanity and to our respective groups.
- Expression: the cliché goes "dress to impress." I would say the most prominent version of such a cliché can be made as "dress to express." To illustrate this, I would bring in school uniforms.

Rendering all students as one with school uniforms essentially is precarious. It makes the devoid of individuality and expressivity.

- Impression: it helps people make an imprint. They say "first impressions are everything." Don't they? Make that first impression on your interviewer, your boss, your date, what have you!
- Communication: I don't think I can stress enough how communicative of a medium fashion is. It is certainly highly visible; it is unspeakable how vocal it is, which essentially ties into the next two on my list. Fashion is indispensably and obstinately revolutionary. It is facilitative for voices of all and any kind and provides platforms of all types in any moment in time and place.
- Voices: voices can resound; they can echo. They are necessitated and mediated by fashion. Not to wax poetic about social media or media in general, but facets of "voice" are substantiated and facilitated by these. Intermixing with fashion, like on blogs of Instagram posts, people are finding voices to launch businesses or support each other through unrelentingly brash and unprecedented times like the COVID-19 pandemic.
- Platforms: Fashion gives us platform. Not long ago, here in the United States, we underwent a monumental display of the #BlackLivesMatter movement (much needed and necessitated by about 400 years of history of oppression and subordination and books like Ta-Nehisi Coates' *Between the World and Me (2015)*, Nella Larsen's *Passing (1929)*, and James McBride's *The Color of Water (1995)* and other factions like the Black Panthers and authors like Alice Walker and Maya Angelou.) It was, to me, the widespread realization of the complicated, evidently ephemeral and precarious nature of Black Lives and their susceptibility to brutality in all forms but not only that. They have to internalize prejudice, and a brand I had been heavily involved with, headed by Black owner and designer Brittany Wongus, brought out a t-shirt saying "Being black is not a crime."

- Aesthetics: The main reason aesthetics and beauty are separate in this section is that I want aesthetics to signify widespread beauty and beauty to be a more personalized and heartfelt (perhaps even emotive) concept. Aesthetics **are** affective and ubiquitous. They are literally everywhere; omnipresent. We take them in like sponges, over time and in varying capacities and contexts. The chiefly collective idea is that they translate to lexicons differently but are **universal**. Aesthetics is not the common term used; beauty is, and that is next (and last) on this incomprehensive but once again NONEXHAUSTIVE list.
- Beauty: beauty is always appreciable. It breaks monotony and banality. It may seem overdone, but is it? If someone is beautiful, does their beauty become less attractive and more underwhelming when they are in view? I think not. I think beauty is something we can all resonate with and come back to at all times. Beauty goes hand in hand with timelessness and transience. Something is remarkable when it is timelessly beautiful. That is why we say "age is but a number." Of course, the opposite of beauty is the abject, with Julia Kristeva talked about in *Powers of Horror*, in 1982. If the abject, (or more commonly and less archaically "ugly") did not exist, what would we compare beauty with? What would we conflate beauty? What schemas would we attach to the term?

***MORE MUSINGS:** Can we be surveilled through or because of fashion/ our fashion choices?*

In her book, *Choreographing Empathy* (2011), Susan L. Foster postulates that we are aware of our body. This novel awareness seems to be corporeal. What I take from it is an extensive simile that trembling bodies and orienting bodies are chaotic like violent earthquakes. We are aware of (and in control of) our bodies. We have facets of the body that are disembodied. We cannot materialize the way in which we move through space, and the movements are clothed by fashion. They are tamed. For example, (I know my extended metaphor/ allegory for this is complicated, but I hope to illustrate it here) Muslim women can wear a burkini to cover themselves while doing the movement of swimming. Another example is how, with bare hands or a sheet, men cover the private parts in movies as we see.

Not only are we surveilling and controlling our own bodies *ourselves*, but we are (maybe to an extent, a weighted, speculative extent) surveilled by fashion. I want to resolutely make and postulate this statement, once again drawing from Susan Foster's ideas in *Choreographing Empathy* (2011) and Michel Foucault's views on power and surveillance (Foucault, 1975.) While Foster is ardently saying that we are rendered "cyborgs" and surveilled through technology, we can say wearable technology (Apple Watches, FitBits) track us. Our mobile devices track us in a way that has captivated and piqued my thought, dumbfounded me, and even flabbergasted me. I was online window shopping, as I call it, not looking to specifically buy anything, and moments following that, Instagram endlessly and imposingly flooded my phone and my app with Kenneth Cole slides, which I did end up buying. (They were tastefully edgy with studs and camo print.) Foucault calls for panoptic, circumspect, circumnavigational systems to punishment and power. While Foucault did consider prison as an "extreme form" of discipline (McKinlay & Starkey, 1998), he drew from Jeremy Bentham's Panopticism (1787.) The discussion shifted to how panoptic power is ideal, because the way the panopticon is structured and built, the prisoner can see what punishments/ conditions may befall him (or her.) In Foucault's view, we humans innately spend time (and socialize ourselves) under power and surveillance (I.E: panopticons.) It is manifest in modern society (Foucault, 1975.) I relate this to fashion, mainly because fashion is evolving and modernizing and profuse at setting the standard for what is cool or what is trending. In modern society, power, surveillance, and fashion interact and have interplay. Fashion stratifies by power, but more critically and relevantly, it limits us and makes us either advantageously or disadvantageously self-conscious, in turn heightening and teasing out anxiety at the same time.

INSPO & STYLE: Our Inspiration and Us

Before we talk about anything that **inspires** us, we need to talk about sense of self. It is the soul of style. It is the heart of style, not just a prerequisite. We need to know and embrace our every nuance, subtlety, and intricacy first, so we can self-realize and self-actualize. To have an adequate and proper sense of self, we need to be aware and acquainted with our own self but also with our surroundings. Alluding back to experiencing fashion actively, or with conviction, you can't take NO for an answer. You need to know yourself so you can cultivate (not develop) your natural, or innate, style persona. Style persona and style personality can be confused but never interchangeable. Personality is your traits or characteristics, principally projecting from your thinking and psyche while persona is the character you project out, and in fashion this is vital. It is the person you are (**uniquely YOU**) and own.

From my perspective, inspiration encompasses three building blocks: intent, aspiration (what look you are going for/ trying to emulate), and influences (these are typically external and trickle into the look.) Now you may be wondering why I am using the word "look." The simple and rough answer to that is that diction **matters.** Let me elaborate. If I said outfit, that means the apparel and accessories that went into the look. Look is more encompassing and takes into consideration the confidence the wearer is projecting and the extrinsic influence that is radiating from the choices that went into the look at hand.

Inspiration is a broad term indeed. It is a common term. It is sometimes shortened to "inspo." I don't know what the protocol for words is, but this one should be in the dictionary or thesaurus for the entries on inspiration. It is the "in vogue" word for inspiration. It is the shorthand; we use shorthand predominantly, perfunctorily, and profusely, especially when texting or Whatsapping; what have you. Inspo takes form our lived and envisioned fashion and experiences. Aspiration can be stretched here to mean not dreams, (which I have always conflated it with), but just the goal for the look (what the wearer wanted to look like), of course, as you might see this requires care and effort on the part of the wearer; it is not supposed to be a passive term. Aspirations are usually proactive anyway, but inspiration can exist without this. Inspiration, incidentally, is kind of the "double-edged sword" here. It can be and it can also not be passive or active. Intent is another grey area. It is active but also seeps into inspiration, which can still be effortless. Intent is still prominent. Intent should be a resounding factor in this and should show somehow. It can resonate with others or it can even be mutually or reciprocally inspirational. Intent is simply defined as what is premeditated, right? It is what we envision. It is partly aspirational, but not entirely. Intent has its own facets for us to unpack.

Influences are the extrinsic part of this. We may have a fashion icon that endlessly, inspires us, for example Rihanna or Madonna or Jared Leto or Pharrell. We may have a literary, TV, or movie character that intuitively inspires us. This is redundant, as fashion icons can be actors, musicians, TV personalities, or what have you, but you can have a musician that inspires you style or a music genre that is most symbolic or resonant of/ with your characteristic style or fashion choices. In a nutshell, we inspire with our outfits and looks.

Inspiration can be concrete or abstract. It can come as esoteric (Holland & Jones, 2017.) It can be envision and foreseen as abstract when considering how a trend (for example) becomes realized or embodied, then it becomes more physiologically in progressing way.

WARDROBING AND STYLE

How do we define wardrobing? Is it a complex process that is more mental than physical, or it is equally characterized by both? How intertwined are its processes with style? In this section, I will define *style dissonance* and talk about the investment in wardrobes as well as fashion as an monetary and mental (maybe even emotional) investment as well. This involves attachment to the items we wear and own.

It is not a secret that wardrobing requires investment. I am not just talking about investment pieces, which means an article of fashion that last long and gives you return on your investment. You need to budget, and you need to evaluate. Those are two things to actively keep in mind with the wardrobe. Be **strategic** about your wardrobe, and analyze your lifestyle. Analyze your style personality, which can be sporty and natural, classic and tailored, or eclectic and interlinked. It can be both, which brings in a primary style personality and a secondary one.

Of course, your wardrobe is one of things that depends on your resources. In this regard, we see the Gen-Z and Gen-Y (millenials, which I am a part of) are buying less expensive clothing. Do they know how to make it last? Do they know how to be strategic? These are pressing research questions.

You will want to discard out-of-fashion clothes and clothing that does not align with lifestyle and goals. You also will discard clothing that does not fit, because we change physically and mentally—meaning our lifestyle can dwindle or go up.

To soundly and profoundly find your style—you essentially need to self-actualize. You need to unlock not only your potential (I know that probably sounds cliché), but you need to unlock YOU, yourself. There is a process here that is itself processed.

- VIGNETTES 1. IDENTITY 2. TIME 3. INSPIRATION: INS

IV

Epilogue

I want to conclude this book by projecting trends or movement tractions that have been recently necessitated (not just by COVID-19.) I also want to restate that fashion is idiosyncratic, nuanced, prominent, and prescient. It weaves the world; it inhabits mankind, and it is also woven by the world (yes, pun intended!) I digressed, but first and foremost, I want to consider two main points I have made here, along with help from sources.

1. Fashion has numerous realms that can be studied (some more intimately and meticulously and others more generically and indistinctly):

    - Consumerism or consumer behavior
    - Marketing segmentation (psychographics and demographics)
    - Sustainability
    - Culture, society, and intercultural relations
    - Race, ethnicity, and interethnic relations
    - History of costume and trends
    - Trend forecasts
    - Desire and the body in general
    - Longing and materialism
    - Subcultures and affiliation to groups

2. There are three types of research in fashion:

- Market research: Here, analysis and trends are utilized, I would imagine. It is here that consumerism is traced and tracked and how the market is trending is also researched. The economic conditions are evaluated and assessed. Everything seemingly becomes predictive and interrelated here. Such research inspires communication and liaising between markets and brands, then on another level, markets and consumers; then on another level are brands and consumers. This is what I have witnessed, so it is partly anecdotal and ancillary.
- Visual: One must ruminate on their color choices and their environmental, even non-environmental (internal or cultivated) inspirations. They will summarize these into a moodboard and vision board. This is a process that is painstaking but fun and rewarding. One will want to find innovative and inviting way to entice clientele and costumer loyalty.
- Physical: This is research on fit and sizing. *How will the consumer feel in this?* This is where the fabrics are considered and chosen. You will also ultimately wonder how the garments restrict or liberates your movement. This is the most intrinsic type of research, in my opinion.

Of course, the new "store" is virtual. Shopping has seen a paradigmatic shift, as it is no secret that countless labels and brands have apps for your phone now. As I stated, ShopDisney.com has a focus of its online store now. I feel like this will flourish, even though the shoppers may prefer to have a tactile experience with the clothes. They will want to try them on for size or fit, and this does not happen virtually. They want to feel the *hand* of the garment (Tortora & Marcketti, 2015.) The hand is the physical feel of the garment. I would argue that shopping is also a kinesthetic activity. This is self-evident, due to the mobility one practices while shopping or even window shopping. It is a multisensory activity, and sights and sounds and smells attract shoppers. They inherently and subconsciously are drawn to places with enriching and refined stimulations. Can we get all of that from an app or website or shoppable content on social media? Of course not, and this is the problem that I admit, having been an impassioned and keen proponent of keeping and maintaining face-to-face or in-person communication or interaction.

Future Consumers

With so much going on in the world and so much having occurred in the recent past, like the pandemic, the fashion world is not impervious, and neither is consumerism. The way consumers spend their money and the habits they engage in are distinct when we break them up into profiles. In this case, we have the new nihilists, the reductionists, the time keepers, and the new pioneers. If we pay close attention to these profiles, we can better understand the make-up that our future consumers are made of; this will allow us to better predict the climate and environment in which we all shop and in which we thrive.

The first profile is of the new nihilists. These consumers have opted out of a world of turmoil and commotion, and they are seeking happiness outside the mainstream. The new nihilists are frankly overwhelmed and taken aback by persisting global phenomena. They are independent thinkers: highly innovative and coming up with novel ideas that are outside the mainstream. They are rule-breakers: finding solutions to the world outside the regular and normative thinking patterns. Now let us reflect on these consumers with a few statistics: 57.3 % if these individuals have concerns about inflation and the cost of living, which speaks to their frustration with how to live and how to thrive. They are disillusioned, and 55 % if them in their mid-30's are dissociated with democracy, significantly more than Generation X people or Baby Boomers felt at this age. They face the issue of eco-anxiety: 50 % of young people, ages 16 to 25, feel sad, anxious, powerless, or even complicit in and about climate change. Over 45 % say their daily life and functioning are negatively impacted by the thought and advent of climate change.

Next, another profile of future consumers is the reductionists, who mainly crave human community and connection. Things have undoubtedly gone out-of-scale, and these individuals would like to restore the world to a human scale, where things aren't so big and fast. They prefer tangible over digital concepts and things and see the impact screens have had on people. They have a heightened sense of their impact on the world and they feel a communal sense that economic growth should be a means to support people and the planet. Time-saving should be ethical and sustainable, as they claim, with fairly paid workers and business models. They value kindness and integrity and would like to see it reciprocated in the world's milieu. They are essentially selfless, valuing other-care over self-care, as reflected by more than 200 studies. They want services like FairBnB and their commission fee to help local community projects and delivery co-op in the United States to have a monthly membership so they can provide drivers with wages and benefits. They reject overconsumption by avidly supporting local businesses with 64 % buying locally since the pandemic. An estimated 60 % of greenhouse gas emissions are projected by 2030 due to the production of textiles.

Third, we have the time-keepers who are essentially "memory-makers" and view time as the most valuable resource. They can simply spend time, but they want to do more; they want to invest it appropriately to enrich their lives. They want to add value to their worlds, rallying against social media culture. They focus on meaning-making and rituals every day to enliven and enrich their lives. They want schedules to fit around people and not people working around schedules and do not pay much attention to age, fostering intergenerational friendships. These consumers want to also see time as money or a monetary investment. They understand time's monetary value, and one cannot waste their time or will have to compensate or pay. Quality is much more important than quantity for this group, as they value meaning and relationships as lasting over material possessions. They can be found slow cooking or long-form reading and value a work-life balance. In a study, 252 % of more time was spent in weekly Microsoft Teams meetings in 2022 as opposed to 2020. As for intergenerational friendships, 37 % of adults in the US have a close friend at least 15 years older or 15 years younger than they are, and 20 % of the intergenerational friendships have lasted longer than 20 years. These consumers have a desire for inclusivity; in fact, 58.6 % of Generation X or Baby Boomers report that they do not see their group represented at scale in fashion marketing. They focus on ageing better—in fact—one in six people will be over the age of 65 by 2050, up from one in 11 from 2019. They also put emphasis on wellness, where it is reflected in 79 % saying that wellness is important, and 42 % see it as a top priority.

Next is the new pioneer. These consumers are compared to light bulbs—where they need to be "switched on." You need to pique their interest with new ideas and problem-solving products that make worlds and spaces—physical and virtual—better for all. The new pioneers are movers and shakers who make opportunities. They thrive on change and novel ideas. They live dually in the physical and digital world, seeking to bridge the gap between both of them. Here there are the thinkers, technologists, And the urban planners who are building new worlds, whether they are building physical urban places that have better functions (like smart cities and inclusive transit) and/ or safer spaces in the metaverse. The pioneers, essentially, can be attributed to creating an ideal online presence and using it to open a physical store (or the other way around.) They are geared to be leaders (regardless of their area of expertise) and are motivated by the need to make an impact and imprint in and on the world. They are generally attracted to products and services that inspire them and let them move seamlessly between different worlds and spaces, whether as digital nomads or different platforms in a virtual team.

Pioneers crave solutions to improve the world. These can manifest themselves as universal designs that can be used by people of varying ages and abilities or more personalized products and services that will be loved for longer and be wasted less. These inquisitive, curious consumers are equally comfortable in the worlds—both physical and digital—and for them, purpose always is more important than the platform. They can be found combining their leisure activities with serious intent. An example is decentralized social media that redirect control to the content creators or digital twins and avatars that solve real world problems through virtual simulations. They can even be found engaging in on-the-ground activities such as Repair Together to stage 'clean-up' raves in Ukraine to restore war-torn locations. Nineteen percent of these consumers have engaged in metaverse opportunities, purchasing virtual goods such as in -game skins or digital fashion items. They built better spaces; 57 % of people across eight European cities want to replace parking space with greenery; 32 % of these consumers want places to rest, and 28 % want wider sidewalks.

These consumers, and we in general, do not exist in a vacuum. We are continuously impacted by interacting and intertwined forces, trends, and our own habits. These forces are also interdependent, as they affect each other. We see internal and external forces: internal ones being our habits and thinking and external forces being trends, occurrences, or others' habits in the word at large. An example of the forces engaging with each other, as they constantly do, is the economy and the environment. They influence each other and impact each other. They essentially cannot exist without each other. When one is concerned about the economy, they may be more motivated to act on the environment. In general, the environment is a general concern for all of these groups of consumers; the reductionists want to support the planet by having workers fairly paid and the business models to be just as well. The time-keepers want to enrich their experiences with rental or fractional ownership models. The new nihilists are overwhelmed by the global problems; 57.3 % are concerned about costs of living, and 50 % admit that the feel sad, anxious, powerless, helpless, or complicit about and in climate change. The new pioneers focus on the intangible and tangible environments. They live in both and are steeped in both, equally. They want to make safer and better environments in both of these domains. They embody pushing boundaries and epitomize innovation and discovering spaces further—again, both material and immaterial. They adopt emerging trends and are always ready to embrace novel and innovative ideals and experiences. They are driven and gravitate towards forward-thinking brands and appreciate when brands foster and embrace creativity, provide opportunities for personalization, and encourage people to express themselves (Indian Designs Exports Private Limited, 2023.)

As a world, we have endured various tragedies recently, like mass shootings and a worldly pandemic. Whether we consider COVID-19 or mental illness, we see that some occurrences are deeply impactful upon the world while others are not so much. Either way, we will look forward to new people using their heart and minds to navigate an ailing and broken world and fashion milieu and consumerism. Whether a person is a new nihilist, a reductionist, a time-keeper, or a new pioneer, they are seeking some kind of presence and meaning in their lives to enrich, enliven, and enhance them. In 2025, these are the consumer profiles that will come up for us to study. We know basically what we need to about them to anticipate their behavioristic habits and consumeristic habits. What tomorrow holds is uncertain but also exciting, and it is helpful to have this predictive information on hand.

General prevailing themes are consciousness and conscientiousness about the environment. These consumers will all embrace creativity in varying forms and facets and think "outside the box." They will have driven but different approaches toward consumerism.

EPILOGUE

V

Author's Note

Why is it important to be "stylistic about style?"
First and foremost, let us elucidate and define the phrase. Being stylistic about style means to be intuitive and observant about fashion and its ramifications. It means to incessantly probe and be piqued by the realm of fashion. We need to be inquisitive and perceptive about fashion. This might sound jargonistic, so let us move onto more targeted, specific details and nuances of the subject.

We question because we want to know, or do we? Nowadays it has become more complex to question ideas and arts around us. We want to know why, not how. We want to be deep into the subject to get a deeper, more circumspect meaning.

I mainly use the term **stylistic** to point to/ refer to research. Being stylistic can mean being programmatic or systemic, thus leading to questioning again. We question others' style or the style of the social hour. We can question the arts and find out how our society or individuals think on varying levels and why they think this way.

Researching fashion can be photographing outfits and seeing what inspired the person to dress that way for the day, aesthetically and philosophically and as a personal choice. It is evidently more and more vital to probe our arts since they trickle, directly and largely, into fashion. Fashion is on of the arts and is particularly evolutionary. It has its ins-and-outs. Probing all of this will tell us about a person's, or more collectively, people's psyches and a society's norms, mores, and ways of thinking.

We can authenticate and validate fashion's dire conversations further, aside from just giving them prominence or perpetuating them. We can go through distinguishing embodied and disembodied aspects; elucidating what is elusive, ephemeral, or just plain hard to see. We can use theories like role theory, dramaturgical approach, and symbolic interactionism (Miller-Spillman and Riley, 2019.) With role theory, describe how one occupies society and how fashion plays into their roles and regulations. With the dramaturgical approach, we can uncover and evaluated how performative and multifaceted fashion is in its history and span. We can see how people feel in Disneybound or cosplay, for example. It is dire to open these doors and possibilities to researching fashion and its theatrical components. People use symbols to communicate just about everything. Symbols are verbal and non-verbal. When attaching any meaning to something, we are interacting symbolically. It is important that we use this sociological theory, along with psychological, psychosocial, anthropological, and other fields of theories to approach the often and characteristically gaudy or resplendent, enriching and incredibly vivacious world and realm(s) of fashion.

There are some prerequisites to being a fashion researcher—or at least a devoted one. Anyone can research fashion—but to be sound, of course, a prior disposition and attachment to fashion is key. You should be well-versed before making judgements that are impartial, empirical, and encyclopedic. You should be able to get immersed and should be innovative as a thinker and researcher. These are basic and exhaustive observations that can apply to being a creative researcher and out-of-the-box, critical, deductive thinker. Once you connect with fashion, ideas will come to you flourishingly, meaningfully, and seamlessly. You will be able to use all kinds of reasoning, and you will "see" fashion beyond its aesthetic qualities. It will come to you as an inward and outward state—a mode of connecting with your inner self and the outer world.

Always remember that you do need to be resilient and perseverant and open to new horizons the research piques. It begets further opportunities for broadening horizons and research as well. Research opens itself up the more it is done. It can snowball, but it is not meant to stonewall. In other words, do not be daunted or overwhelmed and always be ready to use the researching brain. In research, you can stumble upon much uncertainty, which can even be beneficial as aforementioned; know that this is actionable and allows insight; it is not nothingness. It is also not be confused with unknowingness.

References/ Works Cited

Adorno, T. W., & Rabinbach, A. G. (1975). Culture industry reconsidered. *New German Critique*, (6), 12-19.

Bentham, J. (1787). Panopticon: or, the inspection-house.

Berger, J. (2016). *Contagious: Why things catch on*. Simon and Schuster.

Brennen, B. (2017). *Qualitative research methods for media studies* (2nd ed.). New Routledge.

Clodfelter, R. (2018). *Retail buying: From basics to fashion*. Bloomsbury Publishing USA.

Chen, Y. W., & Lin, H. (2016). Cultural identities. In *Oxford Research Encyclopedia of Communication*.

Crane, D., & Bovone, L. (2006). Approaches to material culture: The sociology of fashion and clothing. *Poetics, 34*(6), 319-333.

Cultural Appropriation. (n.d.). In *Cambridge Dictionary*. Cambridge, England, UK: Cambridge University Press.

Franklin, C. (2019). *Fashion: The Definitive Visual History*. Dorling Kindersley Ltd.

Foster, S. (2011). *Choreographing empathy: Kinesthesia in performance*. Routledge.

Gramsci, A. (2010). Intellectuals and hegemony. *Social theory: The multicultural and classic readings*, 263-265.

Hall, S. (2001). Encoding/Decoding. *Media and Cultural Studies: Keyworks, 2*, 163-174.

Foucault, M. (1975). Discipline and punish. *A. Sheridan, Tr., Paris, FR, Gallimard.*

Holland, G., & Jones, R. (2017). *Fashion trend forecasting.* Laurence King.

Kadolph, S. J. (2010). *Textiles* (11th ed.). Prenctice Hill.

Kawamura, Y. (2018). *Fashion-ology: an introduction to fashion studies.* Bloomsbury Publishing.

Kawamura, Y. (2020). *Doing research in fashion and dress: An introduction to qualitative methods.* Bloomsbury Publishing.

Miller-Spillman, K. A., & Reilly, A. (2019). *The meanings of dress.* Fairchild Books.

Motz, L. (1984). The Winter Goddess: Percht, Holda, and Related Figures. *Folklore, 95*(2), 151-166.

Ries, A., & Trout, J. (2001). *Positioning: The Battle for Your Mind.* New York, NY: McGraw-Hill.

Sontag, S. (1994). *Against interpretation.* London: Vintage.

Stone, E., & Farnan, S. A. (2018). *The dynamics of fashion.* Bloomsbury Publishing USA.

Tortora, P. G., & Marcketti, S. B. (2015). *Survey of Historic Costume* (6th ed.). London, UK:
Bloomsbury.

Trousdale, G., & Wise, K. (1991). Beauty and the Beast. Buena Vista Pictures.

Wolfe, M. G., & Wolfe, M. G. (2019). *Fashion marketing & merchandising.* Tinley Park, IL: The Goodheart-Willcox Company.

AUTHOR BIO

Umar Siddiqui graduated from the University of California, Riverside with a bachelor of arts in Media and Cultural Studies and a Master's of Arts from California State University, Northridge. He is currently finishing up his AA in Fashion Merchandising at Fullerton College and volunteers at Fashion Revolution USA. He loves everything Disney and fashion and dabbles regularly in fitness. He likes the beach and waterparks but is a fall and winter person.